MOVING
MOUNTAINS

MOVING MOUNTAINS

The Power of Main Street Americans to Change Our Economy

Janice Shade

191 Bank Street
Burlington, Vermont 05401

Copyright © 2020 by Janice Shade

All rights reserved. No part of this publication may be reproduced, distributed, or transmitted in any form or by any means, including photocopying, recording, or other electronic or mechanical methods, without the prior written permission of the publisher, except in the case of brief quotations embodied in critical reviews and certain other noncommercial uses permitted by copyright law.

Onion River Press
191 Bank Street
Burlington, VT 05401

ISBN: 978-1-949066-37-1 paperback
ISBN: 978-1-949066-38-8 eBook

Library of Congress Control Number: 2020902672

For Courtney

Contents

FOREWORD *by Michael H. Shuman*		ix
INTRODUCTION		1
Chapter 1:	Future Capital Part I	13
Chapter 2:	The True Story	25
Chapter 3:	Ownership vs. Control	49
Chapter 4:	Lifestyle is Not a 4-letter Word	61
Chapter 5:	Money & Gender Bias	81
Chapter 6:	Origins of Crowdfunding	97
Chapter 7:	The Future of Crowdfunding	119
Chapter 8:	Future Capital Part II	139
Chapter 9:	A Call to Action	157
Chapter 10:	Manifesto	173
ACKNOWLEDGMENTS		195
ENDNOTES		201
ABOUT THE AUTHOR		211

Foreword

Deep in the second half of this book is the statistic that Americans have nearly $57 trillion in stocks, bonds, mutual funds, pension funds, and insurance funds—and very little of it is invested in the locally owned businesses we love and we know are critical for community prosperity and well-being. Put another way, we are our own worst enemy. As long as we fail to invest in the businesses, projects, and people in our communities, we will fail to solve the essential challenges of economics, sustainability, and social justice in our backyards.

Janice Shade takes this argument deeper by pointing out that existing funders of local business—big banks, angels, venture capitalists, even many "impact investors"—are reluctant to support "lifestyle businesses." The term is meant to belittle any entrepreneur who—horrors!—wants to run a business, not to flip it for a gazillion dollars, but to lead a decent life while employing people and contributing to the local economy. Professional investors are now looking for a quick buck at the expense of everyone else's well-being. By starving promising businesses before they can succeed, especially those started by women and people of color, our existing financing system is short-changing the real economy, and exacerbating the yawning gap between rich and poor in our country. Emerging grassroots investment options, some of which Shade has pioneered, are providing another path, but walking that path requires all of us to do more work finding and vetting companies that is beyond our capabilities. Thus far, at least.

With more lives than a cat, Shade's experiences give her observations enormous persuasive power. She was marketing director for Seventh Generation in its early years. She created a promising soap company, TrueBody, that was prematurely killed by her venture partners. She consulted with other small businesses to learn how to find better capital sources, and created an important crowdfunding platform in Vermont, Milk Money, to facilitate grassroots investing. Now she is engaged in the critical work of educating small businesses and grassroots investors on how to do local investment effectively. And throughout this time, she has strived to lead a good life, as a spouse, as a mother, and as a good neighbor.

Her story, in the end, is our story. It's a story about how the system, contrary to its mythology, is rigged against the most creative and enterprising people in our society. And her ideas about how we fix our broken system are well worth heeding. Every entrepreneur and investor in American—in short all of us—should read, enjoy, and learn from this important book.

Michael H. Shuman
December 2019

Introduction

Let's start with this crazy thought: Let's think of money as a means of creating relationships and as an intermediary between human beings rather than a possession to be accumulated, counted, invested, and spent. This goes back to the roots of money where its original function was as a medium of exchange. Whether it took the form of cowrie shells, a tally stick, actual coins, or some other token of value, its main function was to facilitate the evolution of civilization when it became unwieldy to use the barter system as a way to trade a surplus of what you'd created for something else that you needed. While bartering is making a much needed comeback in today's economy, our lives are too complex for it to ever be the sole means of exchange. In fact, there is no evidence of a society, historical or contemporary, that uses bartering exclusively to facilitate its economy. I'd have a pretty hard time trading one of my blog posts to City Market Co-op for my groceries. Money will remain a part of our lives for the foreseeable future, so I want to talk about the way we look at money.

My fascination with the abstract idea of money began in the last years of my life in corporate America. In 2006, after 17 years climbing the corporate ladder, I left the gilded cage of full-time employment to explore life as an entrepreneur. Before then, I'd never thought of myself as an entrepreneur. Ever. And the decision to jump off the corporate ladder was not my own, at least not at first. In 2005, I was the head of marketing at Seventh Generation but had been trying for years to create a new Department of Corporate Responsibility within Seventh Generation with me at the head of it. My boss, Jeffrey Hollender, one of the founders of Seventh Generation, encouraged me to write a proposal that he then presented to the management team. In a follow-up meeting with him and our human resources director, Jeffrey told me he loved the concept, but the management team felt the company didn't have the budget for such a move, and since I'd made it clear I wasn't interested in continuing in marketing. . . . Well, you can probably guess how he ended that sentence.

Losing that job was one of the best things that ever happened to me (and I've since thanked Jeffrey for his tough love). I didn't realize how much my corporate career had felt like a cage until I was actually free of it. Even though leaving meant saying goodbye to the gilded part of the cage, i.e., the steady paychecks, benefits, and other trappings of security, within days of that fateful conversation with Jeffrey, I decided not to start looking for another job and to strike out on my own.

Now, when I look back over those first 17 years of my career spent with corporations large and small, I discover that the entrepreneur inside me had been subconsciously rattling the bars of my self-imposed cage for years. In fact, a former colleague who was asked to provide a reference for me in 1999 wrote that I was a "boat-rocker, never satisfied with the status quo." I believe he meant it as a positive attribute, but I remember being, at the time, terrified that the prospective employer with whom I was interviewing wouldn't see it that way at all. (The employer must not have had a problem with it because I did get the job!) Over time, I've come to love my inner boat-rocker and believe it is precisely what makes me an entrepreneur: a healthy dose of dissatisfaction with the status quo coupled with the ingenuity, drive, and determination to create something new and different.

But it takes more than ingenuity, drive, and determination to launch and grow a new business. It takes money. Usually more than a rookie entrepreneur thinks (way more), and the process of raising it often becomes a full-time job. That's not something most entrepreneurs expect. When you've got a great idea that's formed itself into a business plan, then a prototype, and maybe even into some early sales, it's exhilarating. You're on to something good, and you're sure that others must certainly see it too, so the funding will just come, right? I wish I could say that's the case, but for most entrepreneurs—especially the many who don't have a rich uncle (or equivalent) to help them get started—raising capital is a time-consuming and frustrating, but oh-so-necessary process.

On top of all that, not all start-up funding is created equal. The type and source of capital that you bring into your business is possibly more important than the amount of money you raise. This is not something entrepreneurs want to hear, either. They want to focus on what they do best—launching, team building, marketing, selling, and coming up with the next big idea—not raising money. And when they do think about money, they often don't think about the long-term repercussions of bringing in outside capital. This can be a devastating oversight that leads founders toward an end they never imagined. Such was the case with Ben & Jerry's, as we'll see later in the book. But the relationship between money, individuals, and businesses can also be a promising opportunity.

Money has gone far beyond being just a means of exchange. It has become a status symbol that is represented by the size (or number) of our homes, the cars we drive, the clothes/jewelry/limited edition sneakers we wear, where and how often we vacation; you get the picture. A century ago, it inspired a comic strip called *Keeping up with the Joneses,* but today, we've gone far beyond that because now, we have to keep up with the Kardashians.

This book is for entrepreneurs who want to source money for their businesses in a mindful way. Even more so, it is for people who want to put their money to more productive use. It's for those who have decided how much they need to live a comfortable life and still have some money left over that they'd like to do something useful with—both for their future selves and for the current world. This book is about how your money can create current good for your local economy and your community while creating future value for yourself and your family: to do good while you're doing well.

So let's start with the concepts of saving and investing. I think most people would agree that saving—for a rainy day, for an anticipated future purchase, for the day when we no longer work for a living—is a good and important thing. Some of us are taught the valuable lesson of saving at an early age. Some never had to learn it because our parents or grandparents had enough to pass along a sizable inheritance. And many of us either never got the lesson or chose not to heed it.

This book does not pass judgment on those who do or do not have savings. It's about investing in our shared future with whatever means we have available. Whether it's money, or entrepreneurial spirit, or technical assistance, or a willingness to mentor, or even just moral support, all of us can play a role in creating a sustainable future for the communities where we live and work. More importantly, we can also help create a more equitable future for all Americans.

A Google search on the American Dream yielded several results ranging from articles on Medium.com to blog posts to high school essays, all of which used this wording to describe the concept: the ideal that every citizen of the United States should have an equal opportunity to achieve success and prosperity through hard work, determination, and initiative. I find it striking that the definition uses the words *should have* instead of the more affirmative *has*. I wonder if it's because whoever originally wrote the definition believes, like I do, that not everyone has an equal opportunity. At least, not yet.

The American Dream has been, almost from the start, false advertising. The notion that you can start with nothing but a great idea and some gumption to start your own business, be your own boss, make a good living, and retire handsomely is . . . well, it's really only true for some. Historically, the most likely achievers of the American Dream have tended to bear remarkable resemblance to our Founding Fathers.

I'm not trying to disparage the individual achievement of successful entrepreneurs; I'm merely suggesting it's not a coincidence. Of course, there are examples of successful entrepreneurs whose gender, race, ethnicity, or religion differ from 18th century American leaders, but they are a mere fraction of entrepreneurial success stories, and I bet they'd agree when I say it is inordinately harder for them to succeed. Why? Because a key ingredient to success—money—is controlled by the limited group for whom the American Dream has been working so well for the past 250 years. Again, no coincidence.

By the first half of the 20th century, most start-up financing in the U.S. came from wealthy individuals and families like the Rockefellers, Whitneys, and Vanderbilts. Here, we find the roots of our modern-day problem of the concentration of wealth among the few. While the term *angel investor* wasn't coined until 1978 by a University of New Hampshire professor, the practice of wealthy people funding start-ups has been deeply rooted in the American business system for over 100 years. Originally, the term *angel* took its benevolent connotation from patrons of the arts, specifically Broadway theater, where it was used to describe wealthy individuals who poured funds into theatrical productions that would otherwise have had to shut down.[1] Similarly, in the business sector, angel investors have been the wealthy folks willing to back start-ups, i.e., highly risky, unproven, early stage companies, long before other financial backers are ready to step in. Without them, many businesses would never get past the concept phase.

But there's a price to be paid by entrepreneurs for an angel's benevolence. Investors who accept high risk expect a high reward. The dot-com boom in the 1990s helped drive investor expectations through the roof, and despite its subsequent bust, the high reward expectations still remain to the point where the shark has overtaken the angel in 21st century pop culture as the image of an early stage investor. It has become clear that financial support for new businesses is less about spurring economic growth and more about maximizing personal gain. It's about hunting the elusive unicorn—that one "disruptive" business proposition that will take off like a rocket and get sold to the highest bidder for 30 times your original investment. It is precisely this phenomenon that exacerbates the system of privilege and bias in America.

If you Google business failure rate in the U.S., you'll find plenty of articles stating anywhere from 50%–80% of businesses fail within their first five years. Not great odds. Still, hopeful entrepreneurs continue to try, and hopeful investors keep pumping in money. Why? Is it because entrepreneurs are trying to become the next Mark Zuckerberg, Elon Musk, or Jeff Bezos? These are the role models of business success we're given: the millionaire (billionaire?) entrepreneurs who turned ideas into empires. And on the investor side, we've got the Sharks: Mark Cuban, Lori Greiner, and the rest. Is the goal on both sides of the relationship simply to strike it rich? If so, the American Dream is not only biased; it starts to feel more like the lottery. The odds sure seem stacked against winning, but I'll go so far as to say that they're not stacked equally. Some Americans get much better odds than others.

The ability to take an idea and turn it into a successful business is a path strewn with obstacles. And yes, many of the obstacles exist for anyone who starts down the entrepreneurial path, regardless of gender, ethnicity, education, or social status. Where the dream breaks down is in access to the resources needed to overcome those obstacles. There are some powerful resources out there, not the least of which is access to money to help them get started, to help entrepreneurs achieve their dream. But it's more than money. It is the networks and connections that can help open doors, provide technical assistance, or even just be a source of validation that dramatically improve chances for success. These networks are more powerful than money precisely because a strong network begets access to money. This is where the system becomes inequitable, because the networks that provide the greatest access to money, resources, relationships, and other benefits tend to cater to a privileged few.

I'm not the first to point this out. In fact, in 2017–2018, the media started reporting statistics that less than 3% of venture capital goes to women entrepreneurs and less than 1% to Black entrepreneurs. As a result, a movement is growing to bring more women and people of color into venture capital as investors. This is a positive step to be sure, but, to me, it smacks of rearranging deck chairs on the Titanic. In other words, too little, too late. The point is not that we need more venture capital, not even different, more diverse venture capital. I believe the venture capital system (and I include angel investing with it) is contributing to our lopsided American Dream. Instead of trying to fix angel and venture capital, I'm proposing a new system to replace it.

We have the power to change the money system and, thereby, the U.S. economy. For much of the past 40–50 years, we have abdicated our power over our money to big banks and Wall Street, and in so doing, we have allowed them to perpetuate a system of privilege and bias. The way we change this system is to take back our money and demand that it be used in ways that are consistent with our personal values. An easy first step is to bring our money closer to home by banking with a locally owned bank or credit union where it will be put to work in the form of small-business loans, home mortgages, and other projects right in our own communities. But a far bigger impact will be achieved when we can start to do the same with our investments.

Without a system for local investment, money tends to flow out of the local economy to Wall Street investments, which leads to an exacerbated concentration of wealth and a greater divide between gentrified and marginalized areas. A potentially bigger problem is that in communities where there is plenty of entrepreneurial spirit but little access to appropriate capital, we often see a brain drain as prospective entrepreneurs move to areas with a perceived abundance of capital to start their businesses. Or, the would-be entrepreneurs let their dreams die and take unfulfilling jobs just to survive.

I believe there is a sleeping giant of patient, local-minded investment capital that is waiting to be awoken to the possibilities arising from the regulatory changes and innovation spurred by the JOBS Act of 2012. The emergence of equity crowdfunding at the state and national level between 2011–2019 has opened the door for broader access to local investment opportunities for all Americans. It has been an exciting and powerful experiment, and I've had the privilege of being a part of it from the very early days. Much is working, but more needs to evolve. We need more options. That's what I and many others continue to work on. We are creating new ways for millions of us to make small but important changes with our money. If enough of us make these changes, together we can move mountains.

Chapter 1

Future Capital Part I

I was born at the leading edge of Generation X, the so-called forgotten generation. However, we have at least one important claim to fame, and it's one that makes me so glad to be a Gen Xer: We were the first to grow up with rock music from birth. It has always existed in our lifetime (one of my college friends attended Woodstock *in utero*). I'm not talking about old-timey rock & roll (apologies, Chuck Berry), but the music that was already being called Classic Rock by the time I was in middle school: the Beatles, the Rolling Stones, Led Zeppelin, and the Who. Yes, I realize my childhood also coincided with the era of disco, but, fortunately, I had a young and influential aunt and uncle who introduced me to the Grateful Dead, Pink Floyd, Yes, Jethro Tull, and others at a very young age, which kept me on a pure path of great music.

As a Gen Xer, I'm also old enough to remember (vaguely) the day John Lennon died. And I remember when "Imagine" got plenty of airtime on the radio, but it wasn't until much later in my life that I determined it was the best song ever written. "Imagine" dares us to dream of a better world. John knew that if we can imagine it, we can create it. Along those lines, in the latter part of my career, I have begun to imagine what the world could look like if we worked together to create a more equitable and sustainable money system. Here is what I imagine.

Beth Tudor sat at her desk, staring at the pile of reports she needed to read and summarize by the end of the week. She didn't hate her job, but she didn't exactly love it either. She'd been working at Holland & Sons for seven years and had risen to director of operations due, in large part, to her development of an innovative transport tracking system that saved the company thousands of dollars each month. She was proud of her achievements, she respected the company and its management, and she really liked the people she worked with, but she was restless and, quite frankly, bored. Plus, for months, she'd been cultivating an idea for a much bigger innovation that wasn't exactly in the wheelhouse of Holland & Sons, and she knew the company leadership wasn't the sort to welcome this kind of radical new thinking.

She heaved a sigh and opened up a new Word file to start working on the report summary whose deadline was looming. As she typed "Executive Summary" across the top of the page, a spark of rebellion lit her mind. The next sentence she typed was: *Door Tudor Inc. is an innovative distribution company that combines state-of-the-*

art technology with a collaborative and cooperative business model to transport fresh, artisanal products to the markets that seek them.

Beth had just taken the first step toward entrepreneurship, and she liked how it felt. She also felt the tug of responsibility to her current employer, so she quickly saved the one-sentence document, emailed it to her personal address, and got back to work.

On nights and weekends, she continued work on the plan by refining her distribution model, defining her target audience, creating a sales and marketing strategy, and, finally, building spreadsheets of financial models with projected revenues and expenses for the first three years of operations. She'd done the financials last because this was the part that scared her the most, especially the start-up costs. She figured it would take around $30,000 to get up and running. Thirty grand was scary enough, but what about the financial projections that showed the company wouldn't be profitable until the second full year of operation? "This is crazy," she thought. "How did I ever think I could start my own company?"

She shut off her laptop and took her dog, Baji, out to the dog park down the street. As she half-heartedly threw a tennis ball with Baji, a woman, whom she knew only as Diablo's doggy-mom, walked over as Diablo vied with Baji for the tennis ball. "You look like you're on another planet," said Diablo's mom.

Beth realized she'd been mentally wrestling with herself about whether to continue pursuing her business plan or give it up and find a way to stay happy at Holland. She dragged herself back to the present and said, "Oh. Hi. I've just got a lot on my mind: work stuff. You know how it is."

When Diablo's mom asked where she worked, Beth replied, "It's not so much about where I work . . . I actually have an idea for a new business venture, but there's no way I could ever get the money to make it happen."

Diablo's mom picked up the tennis ball that her chihuahua had just dropped at her feet and threw it back to the dueling pair of dogs. "Have you tried the Moreland Community Fund?" she asked. "I hear they've got a boatload of money that was invested by Moreland residents to help local businesses with start-up money, or loans, or whatever."

Beth recalled that she had heard something about this a couple years ago when there were big news stories announcing the investment opportunity. She'd even thought about investing some herself but just hadn't gotten around to it. That night, she pulled up their website and was soon filling out a form to get an appointment with the Moreland Community Fund (MCF) Portfolio Manager, Jed Granger.

Beth's first meeting with Jed Granger wasn't quite what she expected. She'd hoped to knock his socks off with her disruptive distribution system and comprehensive business plan and maybe even walk out of his office with a check. Instead, he gave her some positive but constructive feedback on her plan and recommended she schedule time with the advisor at the local Small Business Development Center to do a little more work on her financial projections and create a pitch deck. Their discussion about creating a pitch deck was the most promising because it was immediately followed by an invitation to present her pitch deck and revised plan to the MCF Investment Committee. This would be the next step toward securing an investment.

The MCF Investment Committee met three times a year, and their next review cycle was seven weeks away. As she sat in her car outside Jed's office, she pulled out the business card he'd given her for MCF's regional Small Business Development Center Advisor, Stephanie Dunham. She fired off a quick email to ask Stephanie for a meeting, and by the time she got home, there was a reply with several suggested meeting dates. Luckily, there was one offered at 7 a.m. the next Tuesday. She could spend an hour with Stephanie and still make it to Holland & Sons by 8:15 a.m. for a full day of work.

After the first meeting, she wished she could've spent the whole day with Stephanie. She was a hoot! She was supportive, compassionate, extremely smart, experienced with start-ups, and all the time, she was cracking jokes and pulling puns that made the work a lot of fun. Perhaps even more valuable, she seemed to know everyone who mattered to a budding entrepreneur and offered to make connections. Beth felt like she'd just won the jackpot—tons of great advice, concrete next steps, an introduction to building networks, and it was all free!

Beth met weekly with Stephanie over the next four weeks, and during this stretch of time, she received several cold, hard doses of reality, particularly on her financial projections. Stephanie convinced Beth that she needed to double her start-up capital expectations to $60,000 and dial back her revenue projections in the first year to more conservative levels, even though this pushed her breakeven point farther out toward the end of year three.

Stephanie also outlined the MCF process. Beth had obviously made it through the first screening with Jed, who typically chose five to six companies to present to the investment community three times a year. The presentation was presided over by the MCF Investment Committee: five member-investors who'd been elected by the fund's entire investor base to perform due diligence on the fund's behalf. After each presentation, the committee conducted a Q&A session and gathered input from other investors with an app. Finally, they deliberated amongst themselves, and, only then, recommended companies for investment back to Jed who would then make the final decision, determine the amount to be invested, and "ink the deal." There was no set number of investments chosen each round. Sometimes they chose all, sometimes none, but usually they chose somewhere in between. There was also no set investment amount, although Stephanie said historically investments were in the range of $25,000–$75,000. She also highlighted that the committee liked to see at least some capital coming from other sources to round out a deal. She advised Beth to aim for at least 25% of her target amount to come from her own investment and/or a *friends and family* (F&F) investment round.

"Okay, that's all very useful information, and I'm pretty confident that between my savings and some of my family members, I can come up with $15,000," Beth said. "But . . . what will it actually BE like? I've never made a pitch before. What do I say? Do I need a fancy presentation? It's open to the public, right? What if people think I'm crazy?"

"First of all, people won't think you're crazy. In fact, they'll probably think you're very creative and brave," Stephanie reassured. "These are fellow Moreland residents, and a big reason why they're doing this is that they believe in homegrown innovation and want to support the local entrepreneurial scene. They know it's best for Moreland in the long run if the money to support economic growth comes from those of us who live and work here because it'll help keep businesses—and money—here in our community. They want you to succeed because it means good jobs, a vibrant business community for Moreland, AND a good financial return for themselves. That's a win-win-win."

"You make it sound almost easy, like I've already gotten the money and my business is growing and thriving!" said Beth.

"Whoa now, you've still got to convince them that you're investable. So let's get to work on your pitch deck," Stephanie replied. "You'll get 12 minutes for your pitch, followed by 18 minutes for Q&A." They set to work outlining her story and the details that the Investment Committee would need to make a decision. "When all is said and done," Stephanie said, "what they're investing in is YOU, so all this confidence and creativity that you show me every week needs to come out in your presentation."

For the rest of their session, Beth and Stephanie focused on putting the final touches on her pitch deck. Afterward, Stephanie sent Beth home to practice, practice, practice. After a week of reciting her pitch to herself in the mirror, she was feeling almost ready, but she couldn't stop the images of an old TV show called *Shark Tank* from popping into her mind every time she imagined what it would be like. She pictured herself being barraged with questions from savvy and successful entrepreneurs while she stood there like a deer in the headlights. It was just this kind of imagery that took her off planet again while at the dog park a week before the presentation. Diablo's mom (her name, Beth had now learned, was Kieran) sidled up to her spaced-out fellow dog parent and waited patiently to be noticed. Beth was clearly rehearsing something because

Kieran could see her lips moving and her hands gesturing while she stared intently at an unseen audience.

At the end of her silent performance, Beth heaved a sigh, closed her eyes, and upon reopening them, noticed Kieran holding a slobbery tennis ball while Diablo and Baji did the nose-to-tail doggy-go-round thing for the umpteenth time. "Oh! How long have you been standing there?" Beth asked.

"Long enough to believe you've got a very patient imaginary friend," Kieran replied.

"You saw that, huh? I'm actually practicing a pitch before I go in front of the shark tank."

Kieran lobbed the tennis ball far enough away for the two dogs to give them some peace for a moment and turned with wide eyes. "Is that old TV show still on? Are you going on television?"

"No, I meant the MCF pitch day. I took your advice and checked them out. Met with the portfolio guy and everything, and, now, I'm on the list to present to them in a week. But I keep imagining that I'll be laughed off the stage or pelted with impossible questions that I can't answer. It's petrifying!"

"Wow, that's exciting! Good for you! Hey, why don't you practice your pitch on me? I don't have any experience with investing, but I've done some amateur theater, so I can at least give you some pointers on your stage presence."

Beth and Kieran set a time to meet at the local coffee shop a few days later (without dogs) and after several run-throughs, Beth was still nervous but much more confident with her delivery. As the date of the investment committee drew closer, Beth noticed another feeling creeping into her consciousness: guilt. After seven years with Holland & Sons, she felt like she was betraying their trust. She decided to sit down with the owner, John Holland, who was also her manager, to announce her plan and make a proposal.

As she prepared her speech for John, she debated with herself about what was scarier: making this proposal to a known and trusted manager or pitching her untested idea to a roomful of potential investors. In the end, she realized that it didn't matter whether John was supportive or fired her on the spot because she was ready to take the leap. The excitement over her new venture was supported by her gut feeling that this was the right next step. She believed strongly that her business idea would bring some good into the world and that she was just the person to make it happen. Buoyed by this confidence, she decided the best way to approach John was from a place of cooperation and gratitude for all the great training and experience she'd gotten while at Holland & Sons. She hoped that he'd see her leaving to start this new venture as a tribute to his success as a manager and business owner.

She sat down in the familiar chair across the desk from her long-time mentor, took a deep breath, and looked him straight in the eye as she said, "John, I want to start by saying how much I appreciate all I've learned at Holland over the years as I worked my way up through the company. You've built a great team, and I've loved being part of it, but . . . I'm ready for a change. On nights and weekends, I've been working on a business plan for a new way to use technology to support a distribution system that's based on a cooperative business model. It takes the best of what I've learned here without being competitive with Holland, and I'm ready to try my hand at running my own company. But don't worry! I'm not going to jump ship right away. I'd like to propose a transition period, where I stay on and help you promote or hire my replacement, so I can train them and make the transition as seamless as possible for you. Maybe over 6–12 weeks? What do you think?"

Chapter 2

The True Story

On August 7, 2008, I walked into Twincraft, a world-class contract manufacturer of bar soap in Winooski, Vermont, ready for my first production run of TrueBody Soap. As instructed, I'd come dressed in old clothes and grubby running shoes, and before we headed down to the production floor, I shoved my ponytail into a hairnet. When I think back on it now, it's like looking at pictures of myself as a kid: I had so much ahead of me and so much to learn!

The production line managers at Twincraft were a little surprised to see me there. They said, "No CEO of a client company *ever* comes to a production run." That took me aback for a second as it dawned on me that, oh yeah, I'm a CEO. What a strange feeling it was to realize that I was now actually, officially the CEO of a company that was no longer just a business plan.

The plant manager and his various line experts escorted me through the entire production process and provided running commentary on all that was happening. They even let me pack soap onto the curing racks at the end of the line. Yes, there were a few moments when the bars were coming at me so fast I felt like Lucy and Ethel in that episode when they shove chocolates in their mouth to keep up with the speed of the line. But soap ain't chocolate, so I stepped back and let the professionals do their jobs.

After watching all those bars of soap coming off the line and then a week later (after cure time), watching them get packed into cartons with my beautiful new logo was like watching a dream come true right before my eyes. I had made this happen.

But that was the easy part; now, I had a company to grow.

Within three months, I gained distribution for TrueBody Soap in most of the natural food co-ops in Vermont and New Hampshire and landed my first really big break by getting into the North Atlantic division of Whole Foods Market. All of this was funded by cracking open my individual retirement account (IRA), securing a business loan from Community Capital of Vermont, and getting some early investments from friends and family.

For anyone who's tried to raise investment capital for a start-up business, the term *friends and family* is an early addition to your financial vocabulary. It comes from the fact that when you're just getting started, your friends and family are the only people you can convince to help get your crazy idea off the ground.

Unfortunately, the term is usually appended with

another *f* word: *fools*. Venture capitalists and angel investors often use this term when talking with entrepreneurs, as in, "How much have you raised from friends, family, and fools." More often, it's just, "How much F-F-F money have you raised." I'm not kidding, they really say that. All the time.

Over the years, I've become less tolerant of those who insist on calling these early stage investors fools. It comes from the notion that most early stage investors are unsophisticated and driven more by emotion than reason when making investments. It also speaks to the fact that in some cases early stage investors are marginalized by later rounds of capital from bigger and more savvy investors who dilute early investments down, often to the point of worthlessness.

Typical F&F investors are people like my roommate from business school and her dad, the best man at my wedding, and a cousin who came into an unexpected inheritance—just to name a few. All in all, 12 friends and family members accounted for just over 25% of the total amount I raised over five years, and most of that was invested at the very beginning. This was the money that helped me make those first bars of soap and get the company launched. They believed in me and my crazy idea, and I couldn't have gotten as far as I did without them. It is insulting to call them fools.

Without F&F investors, a lot of successful businesses would never get past the idea stage. A lot of innovative products and services would still be just a dream rattling around in a frustrated entrepreneur's head instead of breaking into the market, where they might do some good. Plain and simple, F&F investors support and encourage creativity in our economy.

What I found really surprising about my friends and family is that in almost every case, I never asked them to invest; they offered it up! For example, in two instances, I sought out successful entrepreneurs who just happened to be friends and/or former colleagues in order to ask advice on how to raise money. One was my old boss, Jeffrey Hollender, cofounder of Seventh Generation, and the other a friend from business school, Seth Goldman, cofounder of Honest Tea (he had just sold 40% of his company to Coca-Cola). I admit I had an ulterior motive in asking their advice: I was hoping they might introduce me to investors in their network. But I was blown away in both cases when instead, they offered to invest themselves.

After having raised a fair amount of money myself now and having been asked by other entrepreneurs for introductions to my investor network, I realize it was much more likely that Jeffrey and Seth would invest themselves rather than give me access to their little black books of investors. It's such a hard-won and delicate relationship with investors that you don't want to do anything that might jeopardize the relationship you have with them or (let's tell the truth now) take money away from your own company's future capital needs.

With many of my other F&F investors, the investment simply came out of friendly conversations over the course of time as I talked about what I was up to these days. Here is an example of one of those conversations with two people whom my husband and I consider to be our best friends. (In fact, they introduced us to each other, and we are godparents to their son.) About a year after I'd launched, I was staying at their home in Brookline, Massachusetts while attending the Natural Products Expo in Boston. Commonly referred to as Expo East, it's the east coast half of the largest natural products tradeshow in the country. Over dinner (and a few bottles of wine), we got to talking about TrueBody. I started to notice that my friend, Tom, was asking increasingly pointed and probing questions about my product, about the competition I'd seen at the trade show, and the number and quality of customer inquiries I'd received—stuff like that. He's a fairly intense guy and a very successful portfolio manager for a well-known investment management company in Boston. I figured it was merely friendly curiosity enhanced by his professional acumen. Then the conversation took an interesting turn.

Tom: "Are you looking for investment capital?"

Me: "I'm always looking for investment capital."

Tom: "Do you have a business plan and term sheet for the investment deal?"

Me: "Sure. Do you know someone who might be

interested?"

Tom: "Yes. Me."

Simple as that. And that's how most of the initial conversations went with my other F&F investors, too. But don't get me wrong, the process from there was not a slam dunk. With a few of them, all they needed was the paperwork and to be shown where to sign. Most others (like Tom) dug deep into the business plan and asked many tough but fair questions as they did their due diligence. For my part, I asked them (often repeatedly), "Are you sure you want to do this?" I felt a huge responsibility in taking their money and made sure they knew, in no uncertain terms, that this was a risky investment. I told them to think of it as "going to Vegas" money. In other words, they should only invest what they'd be willing to lose if they were on vacation at a casino.

It really is quite remarkable to realize you have earned such respect and trust from your friends. It meant so much to me that they believed in what I was trying to do, which made it all the harder to tell them, in the end, that I'd lost all their money.

But I'm getting ahead of myself.

By Fall of 2011, after three years in business, TrueBody Soap could be found in 350 stores across the country, including the Fred Meyer chain of mainstream grocery stores in the Pacific Northwest. Did I mention Fred Meyer is owned by Kroger, the largest grocery chain in the U.S. with over 3,000 stores nationwide? This important fact made TrueBody's placement in Fred Meyer a very big stepping stone to the proverbial tipping point where the company's revenues would outpace expenses, i.e., become profitable.

Landing Fred Meyer was my first big break into the mainstream grocery market, and it happened just six months after launch, back in March 2009, at the Natural Products Expo West in Anaheim, California. As its name implies, Expo West is the western counterpart of the natural products trade show I'd attended in Boston when I had that fruitful conversation with my investor friend, Tom. Expo West is by far the bigger of the bi-coastal venues, and is held in the Anaheim Convention Center every March. The exhibit floor is nearly 500,000 square feet—more than eight football fields—with over 3,000 companies exhibiting.

About the only good memory I have of Expo West, beside it being the place where TrueBody was discovered by Fred Meyer, is the smell. Yes, the smell. The day before Expo West officially opened, I pulled my rental car into the parking garage and loaded a handcart with a few boxes of last minute sales materials and samples that hadn't made it into the packing crate with the rest of my booth that had shipped weeks before. Dressed in shorts and T-shirt, ready for dust and sweat, I joined the throng of other people making their way toward the Convention Center. It was setup day.

As soon as I stepped through the door into the cavernous exhibit space, I was instantly overwhelmed by the chaos of packing crates (some as large as a VW Beetle), boxes, ladders, booths in various stages of assembly, piles of furniture, masses of product samples and literature, and forklifts that would skewer you if you weren't paying attention. But then I closed my eyes and took a deep breath. It was a *natural products* show, after all, and the scent of essential oils was everywhere. Every year, it smelled the same, although one year, I actually caught the aroma of a burning herb (that was still illegal back then). Someone was obviously seeking a little mood alteration before tackling the tough job of booth setup.

Unfortunately, after the show starts, the lovely smell gets lost amid the odors of cooking food and 75,000+ human bodies wandering the aisles for three long days. But who has time for smelling when it's time for selling?

That first year, my booth was way back in a dark, lonely corner of the tradeshow floor. (I always picture it as dark, but I'm sure it was doused with the same amount of harsh, fluorescent lighting as the rest of the place.) I truly was at the farthest possible point from the main entrance, flanked by companies with nothing more in their booths than a couple folding chairs and brochures that looked like they'd come straight off a home printer.

With 3,000 exhibits vying for attention, it's

important to find ways to make your booth stand out. And just like in real estate, there is huge power in location, location, location. The good locations are close to the main entrance, or on the end of an aisle, or close to the food companies (not surprisingly, the highest traffic area of the show). Getting one of those coveted spaces means paying a higher price per square foot, but it also has a lot to do with seniority. Since the Expo West folks let you choose your booth for the next year while at the current show, all of the good booth space is booked a year in advance. And since I'd registered for the show only about six months before, I got whatever was left.

I made the most of it though and put 10 years of Expo experience to work, pulling from what I'd learned doing trade shows with Welch's, Nelsons, and Seventh Generation plus every scrap of marketing acumen I had to make my booth and my product stand out. The smartest thing I did was hand out samples. I had boxes and boxes of cute hotel-size bars of soap that my daughters had spent countless evenings wrapping with TrueBody labels. I'd hand them to anyone who walked by and say, "Try my soap. It's better than what's at your hotel." The line was genius and always got a chuckle. I'm not being conceited. It really was genius. People came back the next day and said, "I tried your soap this morning, and I love it. How can I bring it into my store?" I even started handing samples to the folks working in the neighboring booths because they'd rave about it and send people my way. That's how I met Kelly Meyer.

Kelly was a *sales broker* whose only account was Fred Meyer (seems appropriate considering his last name, but he was in no way related). A sales broker is an individual or organization you can hire to help you get meetings with store buyers and to manage the sales process for you. They get paid on commission, which makes them a much more affordable option than having to pay salaries and benefits for an in-house sales staff. The downside is that they often represent anywhere from 5–50 other brands (not just yours), and tend to sell what sells best; they focus their attention—and the buyers'—on the "sure things." This can be tough for a new brand with no track record.

I got lucky with Kelly. He had a great relationship with the buyer at Fred Meyer and, I suppose, felt as much responsibility to her as he did to the brands he represented. Kelly came to Expo West every year to comb the aisles and find new products that he believed would fit the Fred Meyer profile. This was a great service to the Fred Meyer buyer and a huge boost if you were one of the lucky brands he discovered.

Fred Meyer, named for its founder, Fred G. Meyer (originally Frederick Grubmeyer), opened its first store in Portland, Oregon in 1922 with the pioneering concept of *one-stop shopping*. Mr. Meyer's vision was to give customers more reasons to shop in his store than in any other. Before he opened his new store, customers went to separate shops for meat, produce, cheese, and other goods. Mr. Meyer placed these all under one roof and put an expert in charge of each area.[2]

Today, Fred Meyer stores carry all the product lines of a traditional grocery store and also include big sections of what's called *general merchandise*, things like clothes, garden tools, electronics, and home products. Fred Meyer was the forerunner of the Walmart superstore. It was also one of the first to create the *store-within-a-store* concept wherein all the natural products are grouped together instead of being shelved next to their conventional competition. In other words, you would go to the natural section to find Seventh Generation laundry detergent instead of looking for it in the laundry aisle with Tide or Woolite.

When Kelly came to talk to me on the last day of the show, he told me he'd already been by my booth a couple times and taken several samples. "I think TrueBody would be a great addition to Fred Meyer's Natural Section," he said. "Would you like me to be your sales rep and try to introduce it to the health and wellness buyer?" In my head, I was doing a little happy dance, but, outwardly, I remained professional and started negotiating an independent sales rep contract. For an initial 12-month period, in exchange for introducing TrueBody to Fred Meyer and managing any in-store sales/marketing promotions, he would receive 5% commission on every case sold to the chain. Considering that most sales reps charge new brands upwards of 10% commission (allegedly due to the extra work required with getting a new brand placed), this was a great deal for TrueBody. Kelly was true to his word, and five months later, I made my first of many shipments to the Fred Meyer distribution center in Puyallup, Washington.

When TrueBody first launched into Fred Meyer, I didn't have a huge marketing budget to promote the product. It's not like I could run TV ads or even print ads in local newspapers. The only marketing I could afford was quarterly price promotions, which meant putting it on sale once every 13 weeks, attracting attention to the product with the sale tags that dangle off the shelf. However, the following year at Expo West 2010, I got validation of an even more powerful marketing tool—one that I'd purposefully designed into the product from the very beginning. This validation came in the guise of an attractive hipster couple who looked to be in their mid-50s, slowly walking the aisle hand-in-hand. As they passed my booth, the woman said, "Hey, this is the soap we like so much." Of course, I had to jump right into *that* conversation!

"Where are you guys from?"

"Portland," the woman responded.

Since TrueBody was still in an early stage of growth, I ran all of the company operations myself and was intimately involved with processing every shipping label and invoice. I knew my list of retail accounts pretty much by heart. I mentally ran through the list trying to remember what stores were in Portland but couldn't think of any. I was so used to selling to individual natural products stores and co-ops and had only been in Fred Meyer a few months that I didn't put two and two together. So I finally asked, "Where did you find TrueBody?"

"Fred Meyer," the woman said. "I'd been looking for an unscented bar soap, and your red box caught my eye."

Red box caught her eye; my branding worked! This wasn't necessarily a huge surprise—it's exactly what I'd designed it to do—but it sure was nice to get the validation. All the time I'd spent researching the category to identify what the competition was doing and what would stand out before I'd ever made a single bar of soap was paying off.

Another far more convincing point of validation was the steady growth of sales. From 2010 to 2011, annual sales of TrueBody grew a whopping 46%. As Kelly Meyer told me often, "The buyer loves TrueBody!" Luckily for me, the folks at Kroger's national headquarters loved the Fred Meyer buyer.

In early 2011, Kroger decided to consolidate its buying function into the national headquarters in Cincinnati. No longer would the regional chains, like Fred Meyer, be able to make their own independent buying decisions. It would all be done by one buyer at the national level. The good news for me was that my buyer was so well-regarded within Kroger that they moved her up to the big time in Cincinnati. The bad news was they put her on a different category. But she loved TrueBody enough to recommend it to the new head buyer at corporate headquarters once she got there.

At around the same time, Kelly told me he was retiring and suggested I get myself a broker that was based in Cincinnati and called solely on Kroger. He suggested National Marketshare Group Inc., and, soon, I was working with Scott Ruth.

In early fall 2011, Scott emailed me to say that Kroger had invited TrueBody to come present an expanded product line for rollout to their entire network of stores. Being invited to Kroger corporate headquarters was the big break I'd been working toward. A distribution gain of this magnitude—in my case, going from 350 stores to over 3,000—would generate revenues that would finally bring the company to the breakeven point. Not only that, once a big chain like Kroger brings you on board, its competition (like Safeway and Target) takes notice and often comes knocking on your door. I started to believe that a Kroger rollout could trigger an avalanche of new distribution, and then TrueBody would be off to the races.

The category review was set for December 3, 2011. I bought my plane ticket for Cincinnati and made plans to see my family in Dayton while I was there. About a week before the scheduled meeting, though, I got a call from Scott saying the new national buyer was still getting settled in her job and had decided to postpone the category review. The new meeting was scheduled for four months later on April 3, 2012. A last minute change like this is all too typical. Big corporate grocery chains like Kroger pretty much make the rules, and manufacturers have to follow suit.

Frustrated, I rebooked the flight and started reworking my board report for the next meeting of TrueBody's Board of Directors on December 16. I had been looking forward to reporting a stunning success from the Kroger category review, and now I had to explain how this delay would have a significant impact on my forecast for 2012. Just a few months earlier, I'd presented the 2012 forecast and budget and, with input from my broker, I'd forecasted a Kroger rollout for six months after the category review in July 2012, which would have given a big boost to sales for the second half of the year. It created the proverbial *hockey stick projection* that venture capitalists love to see, where your sales go from an initial period of slow growth (ideally short-lived) while the company is ramping up into a rocket-ship trajectory up the handle of the stick. Now, with the category review scheduled for April 2012, it was quite likely that the rollout would get pushed into 2013 to avoid the holiday crush at the end of the year. My hockey stick was looking more like a long, slow climb up a smallish hill.

When I look back on this, I realize the long, slow

climb is pretty typical with companies like mine in the consumer products industry, and, more importantly, THERE'S NOTHING WRONG WITH THAT! Weren't we all schooled by Aesop at an early age that slow and steady wins the race? However, in the world of venture capital, that does not compute. Their algorithm for success is to invest in 10 companies, expect eight to fail (or produce small returns, which in their eyes is synonymous with failure), and expect the other two to strike it big with returns in the neighborhood of 10 times their investment within three to five years. These are the elusive unicorns.

I never wanted to be a unicorn. From the very beginning, I set out to create a company with a strong social mission and a commitment to corporate responsibility. In a statement of purpose that I called *The True Promise* (most of which was written well before I even started to work on the initial business plan), I set this goal: to make products that are healthy, effective, ecologically benign, and affordable, within a business model that creates and sustains a sound, vibrant, sustainable business ethic and workplace. Fully mindful that I was running a business, not a nonprofit, I also included this statement under the "Robust Economics" heading:

> We view money and profits as necessary and vital to achieving our mission, for without financial success, we will not fully actualize

our social and environmental goals. Our customers, vendors, employees, and managers must participate fairly in the chain of commerce, with advantage to all and exploitation of none.

This is not necessarily the stuff that gets angel investors and venture capitalists jumping on the bandwagon with their checkbooks open. In fact, when my financial advisor read *The True Promise*, he counseled me to tone it down when I started talking with angels. He was afraid I'd scare them away with my idealistic views.

I didn't tone it down and even went so far as to get the company certified as a B Corporation, which requires a company to meet rigorous standards of social and environmental performance and to include language in its *Articles of Incorporation* to legally expand its corporate responsibilities to include consideration of stakeholder (as opposed to just shareholder) interests.

Even with all this touchy, feely stuff, investors came on board. I wanted to believe that they were aligned with my mission and values, especially the venture capital funds. I wanted to believe that maybe I was having a positive effect on their beliefs and their behavior and that I was showing them that triple bottom line investments were good business. But in the end, I realized I was deluding myself

It was not a pleasant discussion with my board that cold December day in late 2011. I could tell patience was running thin as they watched the hockey stick sales trajectory get pushed farther into the future. But, to their credit, they realized the delay was due to circumstances beyond my control and resigned themselves to wait.

On April 2, I flew to Cincinnati, and the next morning, I met Scott at his office. This was the first time I'd actually met him in person after many months of working together via phone and email. After a quick tour of his office and meeting his team, we sat down to go through the final details of our pitch. I showed him my new product mock-ups and practiced my pitch a couple times. He pronounced me ready, and we started packing up to head over to Kroger.

Our meeting was scheduled for 10 a.m., but it was only 9 a.m. and Kroger, I learned, was just 15 minutes away. "Why are we leaving so early?" I asked.

"Well, first, we'll have to go through security and sign in, and then we'll be escorted to the waiting area. They notice who's early and appreciate it. So we should plan to arrive by 9:30," Scott replied. "We'll go to lunch afterward."

"That's pretty early for lunch . . . isn't it?" I asked, a little confused.

"We're not the only ones scheduled for 10 a.m. There will probably be several other manufacturers there and we'll get called in one by one as the buyer goes through her list," he said. "We could be first on the list, or we could be last."

"So what do we do in the meantime?" I asked.

"We sit and wait," he said.

Kroger corporate headquarters is a huge complex that includes several buildings in downtown Cincinnati. We signed in and got our ID badges and then followed a security guard across the lobby, into an elevator, and through the labyrinthine halls to the waiting room.

Not long after, two more people joined us. One of them was a sales rep for a Canadian company that made natural shampoo, skin care, and cosmetics. He was very interested in TrueBody and hinted that the owner of his company was always looking for brands to acquire. The other guy wouldn't give any of us the time of day. When I finally got my turn, I was given 10 minutes to make my pitch, show my samples, and answer questions. Then I was back out in the waiting room. It was that quick.

Scott said I'd done a great job, and now, we had to wait. He said not to expect a response for at least four weeks. In the end, it took over two months. I tried to be patient, and I made it all the way to the middle of May before I started pestering Scott with emails on a weekly basis to see if there was any word.

Finally in mid-June, I got a cryptic email: "I've heard from the Kroger buyer. I'll call you later today." Since he wanted to talk rather than just sending the news by email, I couldn't help but wonder if the news was, perhaps, not what I was expecting.

I'll never forget that warm, sunny June day. I was

in my office having a meeting with my two employees when my cell phone rang. I was glad he'd called my cell instead of the office line, so I could take the call outside and get some privacy. I asked him to wait a few minutes as I walked out into the sunshine. I started to pace the parking lot as he began what sounded like a practiced speech.

The news he reported was, on the surface, not awful. He said, "The new buyer really liked what you presented and wants to bring in the line." Euphoria! "But . . ." he continued, "she didn't have enough time to redo her *planogram* . . ." (a planogram is a computer-generated schematic of how products fit on the shelf using precise dimensions to maximize the number of products in a particular store section), "and since she didn't revise her planogram, she's not bringing in any new products at this time. All you have to do is come back and present at the next category review, and you'll be in."

That didn't sound so bad. I asked when the next category review would be. "May 2013," Scott said. My heart skipped a beat or two. That was 11 months away! I felt the energy in my body drain away.

After a long silence, I said to Scott, "I think that news just killed my company."

About a week after I got the news from Kroger, it was time for yet another monthly TrueBody Board meeting. This one had already been scheduled to be in person, so the guys from Boston drove up in the morning. As we sat around the boardroom table at Vermont Center for Emerging Technologies on the University of Vermont campus, I put my best spin on what was arguably good news. Kroger had, after all, given tentative acceptance to a national rollout of TrueBody; it was just for a different year.

There was silence after I delivered the news, and all eyes turned toward the board member from the venture capital fund that represented the biggest ownership stake in the company. He knew the company would need another infusion of cash to keep it operating and to finalize development of new product lines before the Kroger launch. He also had a responsibility to the investors in his venture capital fund to demonstrate a portfolio company's (in this case, TrueBody's) ability to deliver on certain expectations for a financial return within a specified timeframe. Unfortunately for TrueBody, time had run out. He said, "We're not willing to make any further investment. You can try to sell the company or just shut it down. We're out." And that was it.

Even though the company had delivered consistently growing sales revenue, it had not yet reached the scale where revenues would cover operating costs, and cash flow was always an issue. In investor-speak, it just needed "a little more runway" before it would take off. But that extended runway would cost money, and with the stigma of a lead investor pulling out, I'd be hard-pressed to find new investors at this stage. On top of that, after four and a half years of constant fundraising while trying to grow a company, I was exhausted and completely burned out.

In January of 2013, after pursuing a couple opportunities to sell the company that never panned out, I officially closed TrueBody. I'd actually come very close to an acquisition a few months before with another Vermont-based consumer product company. I'd known the owners for several years and was excited about the great fit for both our brands to come together under one organization. After several weeks of information sharing, meetings, and negotiations, I received their Letter of Intent on the Friday before Thanksgiving and scrambled to call an emergency meeting of my board of directors before everyone left for the long holiday weekend. However, before I could make that meeting happen, I got a call, early the following Monday morning, from the would-be acquirer to say they'd gotten cold feet over the weekend and were rescinding the offer.

That's when I knew it was time to give up. In December, I began the shutdown process. The erstwhile acquirer was good enough to help me sell off the last of my inventory through their online store, which helped pay down a small part of the outstanding business loan from Community Capital of Vermont, but it wasn't nearly enough. In the end, I was on the hook to repay the remainder of the loan myself because of the personal guarantee I'd had to make back in 2008 to secure the loan. It is a common requirement for business owners to provide personal guarantees (i.e., put a lien on your home or other personal property) when an early stage company has insufficient history of cash flow or collateral to satisfy a lender. To be fair, Community Capital of Vermont never threatened to repossess my home, although they had every right to do so. Together, we worked out a viable payment program, and after two years, I was free of that debt. However, several of TrueBody's creditors and all of its investors (including myself, as I'd invested a significant portion of my life savings in the company) got nothing.

I was left with a crushing personal financial loss and a lot of time to ponder this question: How could a company with a loyal and passionate consumer following that had posted double digit revenue growth for four straight years and had gained distribution in over 350 stores across the country—including Whole Foods and the Fred Meyer division of Kroger—AND was led by an entrepreneur with over 15 years of experience launching successful consumer products with companies like P&G, Welch's, and Seventh Generation and who'd raised nearly $1 million of capital...how could a company with all this going for it fail?

Chapter 3

Ownership vs. Control

The answer to the question at the end of the last chapter resides in the title of this one. There is a big difference between ownership and control of a company, as I learned the hard way.

Whenever I talk with entrepreneurs about raising capital for their businesses (and I've talked with a LOT of them), most of them think they're going to fund their start-up by taking out a bank loan. It's an automatic response built on the fact that banks are a visible, tangible source of capital and have been for years. They're right there on Main Street, and they're theoretically sitting on gobs of money that they're just waiting to lend to small businesses, right?

There is another important aspect of the lending relationship that drives entrepreneurs and small businessowners toward the banks. A loan represents an easily understood relationship for receiving and paying back money. It also represents a finite and limited relationship that is very attractive to entrepreneurs. As scary as it might be to put up some form of collateral, e.g., your home, for a loan, once the loan is paid off, the relationship is over and done. You are once again the master of your domain. All of this is another way of saying that many entrepreneurs and business owners prefer debt over equity because equity means giving up some percentage of ownership, which in their minds equates to giving up control.

They're not entirely wrong about the connection between ownership and control and are wise to be concerned about it. I say not entirely wrong because there are ways to structure investment deals wherein investors have no control over the day-to-day management of a company and limited control over bigger decisions (like selling the company or firing the founder). However, most sophisticated investors who are making large investments, i.e., venture capitalists and angels, would not accept terms that put strict limits on their control. So I advise entrepreneurs to enter into equity investments with a variation on caveat emptor: let the entrepreneur beware.

Early in my money raising experience, I learned about the concept of *value-added investors*. These investors are the ideal kind of investor because they contribute some kind of expertise along with their money to a venture. For example, a dairy farm in Vermont raised capital to expand its operations to include a creamery for processing its milk into butter, cream, and other consumer products. One of the investors they attracted had once worked for Land 'O Lakes and became an invaluable advisor to the management team as he contributed his directly relevant expertise in operations and United States Department of Agriculture compliance in addition to his cash investment.

I had looked forward to this type of collaborative effort when I brought on outside capital for TrueBody, but my experience ended up being vastly different from what I expected. Unfortunately, I believe what I experienced is all too typical of what can happen when companies bring on outside capital.

I was reminded of this about five years after TrueBody closed down when I attended a function with a former member of my TrueBody Advisory Board. Before I go on with this story, it's important to note the difference between an advisory board and a board of directors. A board of directors is required by law if a company is organized as a corporation. A corporate board has ultimate accountability for the corporation's actions, and they are often described as having fiduciary responsibility. Conversely, an advisory board is not required by law (indeed, they are rare and sadly underutilized by entrepreneurs), and members of an advisory board have no responsibility other than to provide ideas, guidance, and feedback to a CEO. The CEO is under no obligation to follow the advice unless they see fit. Ideally, an advisory board becomes a sounding board to explore big strategy questions and for guidance on tough questions like how/when to fire an employee and even how to manage a board of directors for best results.

This former advisory board member of mine is well-known in Vermont financing circles and is president of an innovative Community Development Finance Institution (CDFI) that takes investments from wealthy individuals, foundations, and other philanthropic institutions to provide funding to Vermont's established food, farm, and forestry businesses (i.e., not start-ups). She and I met a few years before I started TrueBody, and as I prepared to launch in 2008, I invited her to join my advisory board.

Ten years later, in the spring of 2018, we attended an event of the Northern New England Women's Investor Network, where the topic was how to connect more female investors with female entrepreneurs. After the main presentation, she and I beelined it to the beautiful layout of hors d'oeuvres, where, over a glass of wine, she asked, "Looking back since you shut down TrueBody, what would you say was the main reason it didn't work out?"

I didn't have to think long about this at all. I'd been wracking my brain—and thinking about writing a book—about this very subject for five years! I looked her straight in the eye and said, "TrueBody didn't make it because I brought on the wrong type of capital. Period. The expectations of TrueBody's angel and venture capital investors were not in line with my original vision for the company, and these investors steered strategic decisions in, what I knew at the time to be, the wrong direction. In the end, their impatience brought on the company's premature death."

She agreed. During plenty of advisory board meetings, she'd witnessed firsthand my frustration as I tried to manage board expectations while staying true to my vision and strategy. Here's how it all unfolded.

On July 9, 2010, I closed on my first significant round of investment capital for TrueBody. My new investors included a venture capital fund from Cambridge, Massachusetts as the lead investor, plus another smaller venture capital fund in Vermont, and several angel investors. I remember the precise date of the closing because it was my daughter's seventh birthday, and after nearly two years of constant fundraising—in the midst of the global financial crisis, mind you—I had no energy left to be excited about finally closing this investment deal, let alone plan a birthday party. I felt like those poor souls you see crawling across the finish line of the Ironman triathlon: spent, drained, and wiped out. (I did manage to muster enough energy to take my daughters and their grandmother to the lake for a picnic, swimming, and ice cream.)

Within days, I discovered there is something remarkably rejuvenating about seeing $400,000 in your bank account, and it didn't take long to regain my enthusiasm as I could finally redirect my efforts toward implementing the strategic plan I'd been pitching to investors for the past two years. A key part of that strategic plan was to expand TrueBody's current product line from one item to five. In the early stages of TrueBody's launch, I'd been very intentional about using my start-up funding (from friends and family as well as my own money) to introduce one strong product to gain initial distribution. Then the plan was to bring on outside investment capital to expand the product line that would help us gain increased distribution. Now that I'd landed the outside investment capital, I was raring to go.

I knew from my brand management experience with Procter & Gamble, Welch's, Seventh Generation, and others that it takes more than one product to build a brand. More importantly, to gain distribution in really big retailers—Target, CVS, etc.—you need a brand block: A series of at least three to five products that creates what's called a *billboard effect* on the shelf where the package design across all your products sitting side by side works together to grab people's attention. At big retail stores, a single product by itself would get lost on the shelf. This is something that big sophisticated retailers know all too well, and I knew it, too. That's why I focused my initial distribution efforts on retailers that were more open to trying out a single product. I successfully got on shelves at Whole Foods and regional grocery chains like Big Y, Roche Brothers, and Fred Meyer.

However, before I could go too far down the product development path with my newly acquired funding, I had to run big strategic moves like this one past my recently expanded and formalized board of directors. As part of the investment terms, TrueBody's Board of Directors was expanded from three members (including me) to five (still including me). The lead venture capital investor got a voting seat on TrueBody's Board of Directors, and the smaller venture capital fund was given observation rights, which meant a representative could be present and participate in discussion but had no vote. I was also required to add one more director from my new set of angel investors who had to be approved by the other directors. The final two directors were my original guys who carried over onto the new board.

This is all very standard, and I knew it was part of the deal. I expected board meetings to be pretty much the same as what I'd had before just with a few more people, so I wasn't prepared for the major change in dynamics. Board meetings prior to this had been held quarterly, often in coffee shops, and thus, tended toward the informal and advisory. Starting in September of 2010, I was now required to hold monthly board meetings that were much more formal. Agendas, PowerPoint presentations, financial reports, and recorded votes became the norm. I'm all for efficiency and documentation, but I was now spending one to two days each month preparing documents and presentations rather than building the business. But all of that I could have gotten used to if I'd believed it were leading to a productive end.

On September 24, 2010, I walked into that first board meeting with new product development as the star of my agenda. I was ready to move into production on one new product that was already in development and to initiate plans for an additional three products for rollout within 12 months. Instead of getting the green light to move forward, I got pushback and insistence that we needed to prioritize distribution over product development. Quite frankly, I was stunned. No one on that board had more experience launching and growing a line of consumer products than I did. In fact, only one board member had any consumer packaged goods experience at all. No matter how many times or ways I tried to drive home the fact that expanded distribution depended precisely on a more robust product line, I was basically shut down. I finally got them to agree to move forward with the one minor product line extension I'd been inching along for months, but the three "big idea" products had to wait. The minutes of the meeting reflect the board's question as to the "necessity and timing of expanding the product line" and indicate that discussion would be "continued in future meetings." I was directed to "sell what you have" and told "we can talk about new products when you hit your targets." It didn't seem to matter to any of the directors when I said my sales targets had been based on presenting a five product line to big new accounts. I was expected to hit the sales targets set for five products with only two. From day one with this new board, I felt hamstrung.

Over the next year or so, what I'd anticipated would be interactive discussions where I could bring strategic issues and get ideas and feedback on how best to solve them became a recurring session of Janice and the Crickets. After that first meeting in September of 2010, most of our monthly meetings were done by conference call since two directors were in Boston and the rest in Vermont. I would get on the phone and walk through the PowerPoint presentation that I'd emailed prior to the call. Then when I asked for ideas or feedback, the phone line would go silent. Since I couldn't see them, I had no idea if they were paying attention; they could be answering email, or doing other work, or even napping for all I knew. The awkward silences that followed my questions lasted so long that I'd just plow ahead with the rest of my slide deck, and, eventually, I stopped asking for input at all. I started referring to the directors as my crickets because it seemed that was all I heard on the other end of the phone.

I am very proud to say that I did succeed in growing distribution over the next 12–18 months, thanks, in part, to the one new product launched in the fall of 2010. In fact, during the five months from August to December of 2010, being free for the first time of the hassle of raising money, I could put 100% focus on building the business. As a result, sales grew 94% in the following 12 months. Unfortunately, even these great results did not achieve the original sales targets (the ones based on five products), and I never got the official okay from the board to put money into new product development. But being the rebel that I am, I engaged the help of an unpaid but highly skilled intern to develop prototypes and package designs and kept working up new products quietly on the side, which turned out to be incredibly foresighted when Kroger came a-calling in the fall of 2011. Still, it was not enough, and as I look back now, I see the seeds of TrueBody's demise being sown in that first board meeting, where new owners took, in my opinion, way too much control away from the one person with highly relevant experience and skills to grow a consumer product company: me.

Where I needed support was in raising capital and building the infrastructure to support growth. These were the areas where I expected, and needed, and, indeed, asked for my board's guidance. I thought I was being bold, honest, and responsible when I demonstrated my areas of strength and asked for help in the areas where I was still learning. I believed this approach would be more productive in the long run than pretending I was good at everything because no one is good at everything.

However, over the course of time, I discovered this approach was not well-received by the board. My advisory board members did their best to help me navigate the increasingly difficult relationship with a board of directors, several of whom seemed to discount my expertise and ignored my vision altogether. In the end, when Kroger delayed its buying decision, all it took was one director (who represented the venture capital fund in Boston) to pull the plug on TrueBody when he said, "We're not willing to wait another year. Try to sell the company or just shut it down. We're out." He had determined that TrueBody was not going to be a unicorn, and his fund didn't have the patience or the willingness to continue funding a business that wasn't demonstrating explosive growth.

Chapter 4

Lifestyle is Not a 4-letter Word

"The social responsibility of a business is to enhance its profits."
~ Milton Friedman[3]

"There is no business to be done on a dead planet."
~ David Brower[4]

The statements above came from two influential Americans who were born just 30 days apart in July 1912, but miles apart in geography (one from each coast of the U.S.), and light years apart in terms of their philosophies and impact.

The first statement was made by Milton Friedman, acclaimed economist, advisor to Ronald Reagan and Margaret Thatcher, winner of the Nobel Memorial Prize in Economic Sciences, and described by *The Economist* as "the most influential economist of the second half of the 20th century . . . possibly of all of it."[5]

The second was said by David Brower, prominent environmentalist, first executive director of The Sierra Club, and founder of numerous other environmental organizations. He was nominated twice for the Nobel Peace Prize and is considered the "Father of the modern environmental movement."[6]

While Friedman's position on corporate social responsibility is possibly better known, I believe Brower's philosophy will have the more lasting influence. Acknowledgment and acceptance of the reality of global climate change is growing. The increasing focus on human rights abuses in factories and businesses around the world, and here in the U.S., has awoken many to the fact that something's got to give. Despite Friedman's dismissal of socially responsible business practices as distortions to economic freedom because they do not generate direct benefit to shareholder returns, the movement toward socially responsible and environmentally sustainable business practices continues to grow to the point where whole industries have grown up to promote, measure, and invest in it.

Terms like *triple bottom line*, *impact investing*, *ESG (environmental, social, governance)*, and *place-based investing* are permeating even the most traditional investment advisory firms. In fact, in 2018, an increasing number of these firms introduced new sustainable mutual funds or exchange-traded funds, including some of the biggest names on Wall Street: Goldman Sachs, Morgan Stanley, and Putnam Investments to name a few. According to research performed by Sustainable Research and Analysis LLC, an independent research and analysis platform that specializes in sustainable investment funds, by the end of 2018, assets under management by sustainable mutual funds and exchange-traded funds had reached an all-time high of $390.4 billion.[7]

This is a very positive sign to be sure. However, there is a caveat: Much of the recent growth in the sustainable investment market is attributed to the rebranding of existing funds that are simply adopting exclusionary or negative screening practices. In other words, managers of these funds are not necessarily out looking for the best and brightest sustainable investment opportunities but are merely screening out bad actors from their portfolio, e.g., companies that deal in tobacco, weapons, and alcohol.

Where we see greater possibility for impact is with direct investments into sustainable and socially responsible businesses. One of the best examples of this has been the pioneering efforts of Investor's Circle (IC). For over 25 years, IC has helped connect wealthy investors with entrepreneurs of companies with a social mission. According to its website, IC has helped more than 300 social ventures that address environmental, health, education, and economic development and other societal challenges to get the investment they needed to do their work. In early 2018, IC merged with the Social Venture Network to "better equip entrepreneurs, impact investors, and capacity-builders with the resources they need to galvanize business as a force for good."[8]

I explored IC when I first started raising capital for TrueBody back in 2009. While my social and environmental mission were a great fit, TrueBody's size and capital needs were not. The company was still too small (in terms of revenue) as was my *ask* (the amount of money I was trying to raise). Back then, IC was looking for deals upwards of $500,000. (After the merger with Social Venture Network, the minimum deal is now $200,000.) Like many entrepreneurs, I was reluctant to give away too much ownership too early and preferred to grow my company organically. Thus, I wanted to raise money in smaller amounts over a longer period of time. Unbeknownst to me at the time, this put me in a category where angels fear to tread. I'm talking about the so-called *lifestyle company*.

I cringe when I think of the entrepreneurs who walk dejectedly out of the *Shark Tank* studio, often having made some serious rookie pitching mistakes. I was lucky enough to learn an important lesson about the world of angel investors outside the public eye and from a much kinder teacher. He was a retired business professional, probably in his early 70s, and an active angel investor. I'd met him at a pitch competition where I'd been voted one of the top three out of the 15 or so pitching companies. He came up to me after the competition and indicated interest in my deal. We made a date to meet a week later for coffee. I showed up with my polished pitch deck and a well-rehearsed presentation. I had answers ready for the questions I anticipated he would ask about my distribution strategy, pricing model, competitive assumptions, and marketing plan. But before he ever got to his questions, he stopped me in my tracks with an unanticipated declaration: "This sounds like a lifestyle company."

Coming from the natural products industry, I was used to hearing the term *lifestyle* to describe a product's benefits, and I had just described to him my 100% natural product line and all the healthy benefits it offered to consumers. So my response was, "Well . . . yes. I'm trying to help people live a healthier lifestyle through the use of my products, so I guess you could call TrueBody a lifestyle company." He politely masked a smirk, and I'm sure he wanted to pat me on the head in a grandfatherly way as he delivered my first lesson in pitching to angel investors. "That's not what I meant," he said. "A lifestyle company is one where the founder starts a business to give themselves a job. They work there every day, might take a day off once in a while to go fishing, and then maybe sell it to their kids when they want to retire."

In other words, a lifestyle company is one where the business owner can actually have a life while they build a business. Somehow, this seems to imply a lack of ambition to angel investors. I was taken aback by this. All through my pitch, I'd demonstrated how I'd gotten early placement in Whole Foods and then planned to leverage it into national mainstream grocery distribution and, ultimately, into mass merchandisers like Target. I had growth charts and financial projections that forecast over $1 million in annual sales by year three. What about this said lifestyle company? The only explanation I could come up with was that I was a woman with a natural products company—not a man with a high-tech company—and, also, I was a woman with a husband and two young children, which all too often is misinterpreted by angel investors as someone who is just doing this as a hobby.

This was an a-ha moment for me. I quickly learned that lifestyle company is a broadly used term in the investing world, typically with derision and condescension, and is the kiss of death to start-ups seeking investment capital. Angels don't invest in lifestyle companies. Period. They want to find companies with an exit strategy that promises a return on investment (ROI) in the neighborhood of 5–10 times their money within three to five years. In order for that to happen, an entrepreneur is expected to invest every aspect of themselves into growing the company. They're expected to work 80-hour weeks and live on adrenaline and ramen noodles while putting their own "skin in the game" by investing whatever personal wealth they might have. God forbid they have a spouse or a family; these are just a distraction from growing the business. There are no readily available statistics for the divorce rate among entrepreneurs, but it is a common enough phenomenon that Meg Cadoux Hirschberg, wife of Stonyfield Yogurt founder, Gary Hirschberg, wrote a book in 2012 titled *For Better or for Work: A Survival Guide for Entrepreneurs and Their Families*.

To further illustrate this deeply ingrained bias against lifestyle companies, here is another anecdote from my experience with a different angel investor. I don't remember his name, so I'll call him Jim. I made arrangements to meet Jim at a coffee shop near the office of one of his portfolio companies in Cambridge, Massachusetts. When we sat down, he said he could only spare 30 minutes with me since his wife and grandchildren were with him. I didn't know they'd be tagging along when we'd made the appointment a few weeks earlier, and it, clearly, never occurred to him that I'd hit the road at 6 a.m. and driven three and a half hours from northern Vermont just to meet him.

He started by extolling the virtues of his portfolio company that he'd just visited. It was a technology company founded by a guy who "regularly slept on a futon at the office and lived on ramen noodles and PB&J sandwiches." He then went on to tell me of another portfolio company in an attempt, I suppose, to demonstrate that he invests in women-owned companies, too (an anomaly among angels back then, and, unfortunately, still today). This company was started by two (apparently unmarried) women who each sold their homes and invested the proceeds into their company and were now sharing a small apartment in Somerville, Massachusetts.

He never had to say lifestyle company, but I got the message loud and clear that he was giving me an opportunity to demonstrate that mine was not one. I nimbly worked into the conversation the fact that I'd invested most of my retirement savings into the company, put my home up as collateral on a business loan, and regularly stayed up late after I put my kids to bed to answer email while working for three years without a salary. At the end of our 30 minutes, when I thought I'd passed the test and made significant progress toward an investment, he announced that he couldn't give me a decision for at least six weeks because he was leaving the next day for an extended trip to Paris with his wife and would be incommunicado until he returned.

I'd been through the process with enough angels by then to know that if he said six weeks before he could make a decision, it would be more like 8–10 weeks, and then, if he actually decided to make an investment, it could take another three to four weeks before paperwork was signed and a check came my way. So that meant at least another three months of trying to keep sales momentum growing on a shoestring budget, assuming I could get back on his radar after he returned from France, with no guarantee it would ever amount to anything. All the while, I was also courting other angels because I'd learned that you've got to kiss a lot of frogs before a prince comes through with an investment. A rule of thumb for entrepreneurs who are raising angel/venture capital is that for every 10 investors you pursue, you might get one investment. Raising money had become my full-time job, on top of my other full-time job of growing a company. It was exhausting!

Now, I realize there is an expectation that when a company is successful, the entrepreneur will strike it rich alongside her investors. This is the myth of *sweat equity*, and it goes something like this: the entrepreneur will be rewarded in the end for all the blood, sweat, and tears she invested in her venture when she gets the big payday after her company is acquired. Sadly, more often than not, founder's equity gets crammed so far down by subsequent rounds of investment that they often walk away from an otherwise successful sale of their business with not much to show for it. And in the meantime, you can't feed yourself (or your kids) on sweat equity while you're trying to get to that big payday. This often means that, unless you are willing to starve for your start-up, the only people who can afford to be entrepreneurs are those with a lot of their own money to invest or a high-salaried (and supportive) spouse.

The irony of all this was not lost on me at the time, and, over the years, I've recalled this experience as an illustration of how the current investment capital system perpetuates the concentration of wealth among those at the high end of the wealth spectrum. The angel/venture capital system promotes an unsustainable, if not destructive, economic model that is detrimental to the social fabric of our country. It's driven by the fact that angels and venture capitalists follow a *home run model* with their portfolios. To illustrate, let's say an angel invests in 10 companies. Of those 10, they expect one or two to be home runs (aka unicorns) that pay them back 10 times their original investment (that's roughly equivalent to a 900% return). Of the remaining eight investments, they hope maybe five or six will provide small (10%–20%) returns or at least break even, and the rest they expect to fail outright. In essence, they're gambling that one or two of their investments will cash out big enough to make up for the losses or lackluster returns of the rest. Not long ago, I overheard an angel investor rationalizing the risks that she takes with some of her portfolio companies because she'd made 27 times her investment on one of her first deals. These kinds of expectations entice investors to take risks on companies they believe will deliver the proverbial hockey stick growth curve; they're willing to ride out the short end of the stick, where there's flat growth during the very earliest stage, in anticipation of the quick ramp up along the handle toward soaring profits. In a way, the search for the elusive "unicorn with a hockey stick" is a lot like playing the roulette wheel. But unlike gambling where so much is left to chance, angels and venture capital investors influence the odds for success in their portfolios by a tactic I call *feed the unicorn and starve the workhorse*.

Savvy investors do not put 100% of their planned investment into a business right away. They keep a reserve of capital for follow-on investments. Let's say an investor allocates $100,000 for a particular investment. They might invest $50,000 at first and then watch to see what happens. As a company grows and, inevitably, needs more money, the investor can choose to make an additional $50,000 investment to keep momentum going. In accordance with the home run model, angels and venture capital investors are far more likely to make follow-on investments in those companies that show the earliest and fastest signs of growth. Unfortunately, this reality results in many slower growing but potentially viable start-ups falling out of favor before they've truly proven their viability. They are relegated to the dead end of an investor's portfolio, where they receive less, possibly no, follow-on investment, and their failure becomes a self-fulfilling prophecy. Thus, feed-the-unicorn-and-starve-the-workhorse is a model that does not lead to meaningful economic growth because it lacks balance and could even drive the premature demise of companies that, with appropriate support, would end up being good solid doubles, or triples, or even late game home runs.

Please pardon my mixed metaphors above, but I believe they help illustrate a very important point. Angels and venture capital funds often like to tout their investment models as a way to ignite economic growth and innovation. To a certain extent, they do contribute to entrepreneurism and innovation, but I argue that their unbalanced home run model brings potentially devastating long-term effects by creating a capital desert for start-ups that could possibly become stable and profitable companies in the long run but that have more moderate growth trajectories. How many of these companies fail prematurely due to lack of follow-on funding from their early investors or because they never receive funding in the first place? How many become a would-be entrepreneur's aborted dream?

These might very well be the oft-maligned lifestyle companies that are led by passionate, dedicated business owners who want to help their venture grow and succeed over time. These are the companies that are the backbone of the American economy. Between 2009–2011, as the U.S. scratched and clawed its way out of recession, *small businesses*, defined as those with fewer than 500 employees, contributed 67% of net new jobs to the economy.[9] Yet many start-ups that could become thriving small businesses that create jobs and other economic benefits for a community over many years find themselves forced down a path toward acquisition. Or they just don't get funded in the first place. This is how angels and venture capitalists actually erode economic opportunity, not support it.

Also, by pushing the fastest growing companies in their portfolio toward a *successful exit*, venture funds and angels have institutionalized acquisition as the only method for getting a return on their investment. In other words, they want a company to sell as quickly as possible to the highest bidder. While acquisition is good for an investor's bank account, it can have harmful effects on the communities and local economies where a start-up was initially headquartered. Acquisition often leads to local job loss as the new owner (based who knows where) absorbs management roles into national headquarters far away, closes down production facilities, or outsources technical functions to cheaper labor sources offshore. Exacerbating this is the loss of revenue for other local businesses that supplied the original start-up with goods and services: the local bank where accounts were kept, the restaurant on the corner where employees spent many lunch hours, the graphic design shop that created marketing materials. Many businesses—and people—lose when a company leaves town.

All of this has fueled my efforts to find ways to champion the lifestyle companies of the world. I question why it's acceptable, even expected, that entrepreneurs will devote most if not all of their waking hours and their personal wealth to their venture often while sacrificing their health and personal relationships so that a few wealthy individuals can make more money. My bigger and broader reaching question is this: What's so bad about lifestyle companies? What's wrong with a company that grows at an organic pace, produces modest but consistent profits, creates employment for the owner and possibly 10–100 other people, and generally contributes to the economic welfare of its community through local purchases of other goods and services, charitable donations, and other acts of good corporate citizenship? Why is this type of company not seen as a worthy investment opportunity?

At least part of the reason lies in our more-is-better society. Why would you be satisfied with a 10% return if you could double, or triple, (or 10X) your money? We've been conditioned to buy low/sell high, maximize profits, grow or die, and parrot Gordon Gecko's "greed...is good."[10] The underlying assumption with all these is that there's no such thing as too much money. What this assumption means, though, is that our measure of success is tied to an ever-moving target of more, more, more. That's a no-win situation because we never get to cross a finish line; we never get to say, "I've made it." It's exhausting just to think about, and yet it's so easy to get caught up in the quest for more.

So that brings me to another important question: How much is enough? It's a tricky one and oh-so-difficult to pin down because the answer will be different for everyone. I like this definition from Vicki Robin: "Enough is the quality of having everything you need and want, but nothing in excess, nothing that burdens you."[11] It kind of stops you in your tracks to think of money as a burden doesn't it?

Several years ago, a friend introduced me to an exercise where you imagined your life at different levels of annual income and wrote down how it made you feel. You start at $5,000 of annual income and write down whatever comes to mind, and then you do the same for growing increments ($10,000, $25,000, $50,000 all the way up to $1 million). It's interesting to look back on my notes and witness at what dollar level my thoughts went from "Panic!" to "I can breathe now" to this:

> It feels like too much work to have this much money and manage it in a way that is consistent with my values. I'll become married to my money . . . or money management will become my job. Just like having not enough money is hard, having too much money is hard, too. It makes me tired thinking about it. I'd like to have enough to be financially independent, which means being independent from my money, too.

There are lot of other things I'd rather do with my life than commit too much time to thinking about how to spend, invest, give away, or protect my money. That last one, protecting one's money, becomes more time- and energy-consuming the more money you have. When you've got a lot, you become a target. There's a certain truth in Bob Dylan's line, "When you ain't got nothing, you got nothing to lose."[12] There's a kind of freedom in having nothing. I feel a little sorry for rich people who are constantly being hit up for donations and investments. Many of them engage gate-keepers in the form of investment advisors, certified public accountants, and the like, but then you've got to worry about whether they're honest and working in your best interest.

Happily, I'm starting to see signs that the concept of enough is being taking seriously. People are talking about—indeed, workshops are being taught on—the crazy notion of giving up some financial return in exchange for less tangible, more socially-enriching, benefits. Terms like *concessionary returns*, *recoverable grants*, and *social return on investment* (SROI) are starting to show up in conversations, mostly among philanthropic organizations that might be willing to let go of a little financial gain if an investment is in line with their mission.

Let's take a look at what these terms mean. A concessionary return means an investor concedes (or gives up) an expectation for market rates on an investment, where *market* refers to, you guessed it, Wall Street-type investments. In other words, the investor is willing to make a little less money because they're investing in something aligned with their mission. I find it a bit ironic when foundations and other philanthropic organizations use the term because it only points to the financial concessions made by an investor and ignores the concessions to their mission or social values when they make investments in companies with poor records on workers' rights and environmental and other sustainability measures just for the sake of making high returns. We don't say we're making concessionary returns on the environment or on social welfare when we invest in Monsanto or Walmart. It's all about the money.

My friend, Marco Vangelisti, a self-proclaimed refugee from conventional finance, often shares the following story in his workshops to illustrate this point. For 20 years, Marco managed investment portfolios on behalf of large foundations and endowments. One day, he realized that one of the best performing investments in a client's portfolio was a Malaysian palm oil company that was notorious for clearcutting rainforest and destroying orangutan habitat. That's not the worst part, though; his client just happened to be a nonprofit organization founded specifically to protect the orangutan! He had inadvertently helped create a vicious cycle of destruction and ineffective activism in the name of generating above-market investment returns for his client to then use to combat a problem that they had unwittingly helped cause.

Not long after this discovery, Marco followed his conscience and left his well-paying job. He also divested his personal portfolio of all international investments, large capitalization stocks, and mutual funds. He is now a 100% impact investor with a commitment to direct local investing. He is also the founder of Essential Knowledge for Transition (EK4T). Through EK4T, he teaches workshops, offers guest lectures, and facilitates community conversations to empower citizens to align their investments with their values.

I've had the pleasure of hearing Marco speak several times and, as part of the Slow Money Vermont team, helped bring him to Vermont to teach a daylong workshop in 2017. He and I have also worked together on the team that formed the National Coalition for Community Capital, and it was through this work that I first heard him use the term *recoverable grant*.

Recoverable grants were initially created by nonprofits to make investments in social entrepreneurs. The idea is that an entrepreneur receives much needed early stage seed money to get their venture off the ground without the burden of having to make a loan payment or meet an equity investor's expectation for explosive growth (or lose control of their company). At some point in the future, when (and if) the company achieves a pre-agreed milestone, the recoverable grant converts and becomes an investment vehicle with a modest financial return back to the nonprofit organization. You'll notice the *if* in parentheses in the last sentence; the parentheses indicate the nonprofit investor's acknowledgment that the company may never hit the pre-agreed milestone. In such a case, the investment is simply considered a grant, with no payback expectations.

Lifestyle is Not a 4-letter Word 79

Marco, and others, are taking this concept beyond the nonprofit realm and asking individual investors to look on early stage investments as recoverable grants. In other words, asking them to give up (or at least dramatically reduce) the expectation for returns in the early stage and possibly forever. It's an interesting approach, but I believe it's a hard one for many individuals to get excited about.

Conversely, SROI has greater possibility of acceptance and understanding as well as greater possibility of encouraging a more permanent move toward sustainable business practices. SROI is the upside to the concessionary return because it fills the perceived gap in personal financial return with benefits to communities and the environment. The key here is to recognize that wealth can accrue to individuals through means other than an ever-growing bank account and that SROI can take the form of more than a feel-good reward for doing the right thing.

Consider this example. An economically challenged rural region with chronic under-employment, high crime rates, and drug abuse looks to its citizens, local business leaders, and philanthropic institutions to band together in a community investment fund to provide capital to new or established businesses that demonstrate a desire to improve the health and prosperity of their region. The fund invests in businesses that are built-to-last and will create long-term, well-paying jobs; in real estate ventures that revitalize downtown areas with mixed-use properties of affordable housing and retail; and in technology incubators that provide opportunities for young families to stay in the region and encourage science, technology, engineering, and mathematics education in local schools. Over time, the employment rate increases, and crime and drug abuse rates drop. The tax base is expanded by the addition of new businesses and wage-earners, and as a result, property tax rates actually start to decline. Citizens who are well-housed, well-fed, financially stable, and physically healthier are also happier in general. Happier citizens are more productive, and thus, the cycle of wealth circulates throughout the region for increased prosperity for all.

This seems right in line with David Brower's vision of how to do business for a living planet and well worth giving up a couple percentage points on one's investment portfolio. Don't you think?

Chapter 5

Money & Gender Bias

On a cold, gray winter day in 2016, I made my way down Route 100 to Waitsfield in north-central Vermont. There's something magical about the Mad River Valley where Waitsfield is located. Deep in the Green Mountains and home to the legendary ski areas of Sugarbush and Mad River Glen, the valley is an eclectic mix of folksy Vermonters and wealthy out of state residents whose 2nd (or 3rd) homes are tucked away along the mountain ranges.

It was February 17, 2016 which, despite the approaching equinox, is still considered midwinter in a place where the snow often sticks around until late April, and I was headed to Liz Lovely Cookies to meet its namesake, Liz Scott, to talk about helping her raise capital.

By this time, I was three years beyond shutting down TrueBody. After a very short stint as the marketing director for a local sports equipment manufacturer, I realized that my first bite at the entrepreneurial apple had me hooked. I lasted only seven months at the sports equipment manufacturer before I broke out once again from the gilded cage and started planning my next venture. That venture was Milk Money, one of the first equity crowdfunding platforms in the U.S. Founded in 2015 and launched in 2016, it allowed investors of any means, not just wealthy, *accredited investors*, to make investments into private companies. (More on all of that, including the definition of accredited investor, in Chapter 6.) What follows is Liz's story.

At the time of my visit, Liz Scott was still known as Liz Holtz, her married name, even though she'd been through a pretty rough divorce a little over a year earlier. Liz and her former husband, Dan Holtz, had started Liz Lovely Cookies in 2003 in Philadelphia and experienced quick success as they tapped into the nascent vegan/gluten-free trend and gained early distribution in Whole Foods. Within a year, they needed a bigger bakery space and decided to move the business to a place more aligned with their vision for their lives and their company. Dan made a cold call to former Ben & Jerry's CEO, Fred "Chico" Lager, who connected the couple with Robin Morris, an entrepreneur and investor based in Waitsfield. Robin had recently created what is now known as the Mad River Food Hub, a business incubator in Waitsfield. After meeting the couple and discussing the opportunity, Robin made a small investment in Liz Lovely in 2004 and built a 2,000-square-foot space for the company."[13]

Over the next eight years, the company continued to grow despite tough outside influences like the Great Recession of 2008, which hit just as the company had gambled on extending distribution to the West Coast. And in 2011, Tropical Storm Irene devastated the Mad River Valley, literally washing away Liz Lovely's inventory and its newly launched retail store.

Over the years, Liz and Dan funded much of Liz Lovely's growth with capital from community-focused lenders like the Vermont Economic Development Authority, the Flexible Capital Fund (part of Vermont Sustainable Jobs Fund), and from local investors. However, by 2012, as they struggled to match production and infrastructure growth with the demands of bigger, more sophisticated customers, they decided it was time for bigger investment and landed themselves a spot on *Shark Tank*. As they made their pitch on air in September of 2012, Mark Cuban, a self-described "gluten-free mogul,"[14] was the only shark to take interest and asked for a better offer. The couple countered with a new offer that doubled the ownership stake from 10% to 20% for a $200,000 investment, but Cuban declined. Liz and Dan left the tank without a deal.

Whether the disappointing result of their *Shark Tank* foray was directly responsible or not, the couple's personal life fell apart after that, and, by 2014, it ended in a divorce that, according to Liz, "was not in any way amicable."[15] She took over full management responsibility for Liz Lovely, thanks to a founders' agreement that gave her first right of refusal to keep the business. It was a big change for her as she moved from the bakery floor to the CEO's office practically overnight. While getting a crash course on how to run a growing business single-handedly, her biggest challenge was to raise the money that the company still needed to increase production and hire a sales manager to keep up with growth. Her board had told her not to try to get any more loans since she'd maxed out the debt capacity of her balance sheet and new loan payments would eat up cash flow that was badly needed to build the business. This left equity financing as her best option. She needed patient investors who would see the long-term horizon and be willing to take the risk of getting a return on their investment at some point in the future. On the advice of Janice St. Onge, head of the Flexible Capital Fund that had invested in Liz Lovely early on, Liz contacted Milk Money to explore a Vermont crowdfunding campaign.

That's what brought Louisa Schibli, fellow cofounder of Milk Money, and me to Waitsfield that cold day in February of 2016. We had just launched our crowdfunding platform a week before and had an inaugural campaign in the works with another Vermont female entrepreneur who also ran a food-based business. We believed Liz Lovely, with its broad distribution and great brand recognition, would be highly attractive to Vermont investors; moreover, the combined campaign outreach for her business plus the other woman entrepreneur would make for great press coverage for both companies and Milk Money, too. Liz was immediately intrigued by the prospect of engaging her fellow Vermonters to invest in the company, much like Ben & Jerry's had done 30 years earlier with their Vermont-only direct public offering (DPO) to build their ice cream factory just up the road in Waterbury. However, she did admit some misgivings; she was starting to entertain the thought of moving the company outside of Vermont due to the difficulty of finding a manufacturing facility to meet her needs here, and she didn't have the capacity to try to build one on her own. We talked for a while about the benefits and limitations of local crowdfunding, and in the end, she was excited, or perhaps desperate, enough to agree to take some next steps.

Over the next several months, we continued to consult with Liz about a local crowdfunding campaign and helped her test the waters with potential investors at one of Milk Money's Invest Local educational events in June 2016. During that time, she was also pursuing traditional equity funding with angel groups and venture capital funds in Vermont and Boston. By the end of the summer, she told us she'd decided to focus exclusively on traditional capital but asked us to keep in touch.

By the next winter, we'd completely lost touch with Liz, and I only discovered why as I did the research for this book. In late summer 2016, around the same time she'd told Milk Money thanks but no thanks, Liz Lovely had stopped shipping product and closed its doors, leaving a pile of unpaid bills, loans, and investors in its wake. In the words of Robin Morris, Liz Lovely's early investor and staunch supporter, "At the end, Liz just ran out of money. The business ran out of money."[16]

So how did this happen? Here was a company that had pioneered and led the gluten-free cookie category for 13 years, at one point employing 24 people and generating annual sales of nearly $2 million. How does a company with this kind of track record and momentum not get funded? According to some close to the situation, it's because she's a woman. Rumor has it that some of the traditional equity investors she was courting got cold feet because she was a solo female entrepreneur, and, as such, she'd need too much "hand-holding." The underlying assumption being that if she were a man, the investors could theoretically trust him to run and grow a company on his own, but a woman would need closer oversight and help. Whether the rumor is true or not, for whatever reason, they did not invest, and Liz was left high and dry.

Where would Liz Lovely be today if Liz had been able to raise the $150,000–$200,000 she needed to hire a sales manager to focus on growing revenue while she managed the rest of the business? Unfortunately, we'll never know. Another potentially fruitful business died on the vine.

Unfortunately, the Liz Lovely story is not an isolated case. In January 2018, *Fortune* magazine reported a study by Pitchbook, a mergers and acquisitions, private equity, and venture capital database, that showed female entrepreneurs received about 2.2% of the $85 billion invested by venture capitalists in 2017 versus the roughly 79% received by all-male teams. The study goes on to say that not only are there fewer deals done with women entrepreneurs, the deals also tend to be smaller in terms of dollars invested. The article does point to a supposed silver lining, stating "with the exception of 2014, 2017 marks the largest percentage of total venture dollars that has gone to female founders since PitchBook started tracking the data in 2006."[17] Hooray, we're up to 2.2%. (Is my sarcasm coming through?)

Clearly, gender bias is an issue when it comes to investment capital. The good news is that awareness is building and venture capital funds are starting to take action. A 2017 report by *TechCrunch* reported these signs of progress:

- Among the top 100 venture firms, women comprise 8% of all partners (up from 7% in 2016).
- Eight firms in the top 100 added a female partner for the first time.

- Women now hold 15% of partner roles at accelerators and corporate venture firms.
- Women founded 16 micro-venture funds between 2014 and 2017, which is 21% of all new firms in that category.[18]

But are more female venture capitalists really the answer? Is a lack of venture capital for women entrepreneurs even a problem in the first place? Maybe the problem is that the types of businesses women tend to create are not a good fit for the venture capital model. I'm referring to the misunderstood and often overlooked lifestyle company, of course, but also about the fact that women tend to start businesses in different industries from men.

According to a recent article in *Forbes*, "Compared to men, women start a much higher percentage of businesses in wholesale and retail, as well as in health, education, government, and social services. Only 3 percent of women entrepreneurs start information and communications technology businesses."[19] A 2016 Kauffman Foundation compilation report titled *Research on Gender and Entrepreneurship* provides further insight into the disconnect between women-led businesses and angel/venture capital investment. It states that women-led businesses tend to be:

- smaller on average
- financed at a lower rate

- less profitable
- slower to grow
- home-based
- in female-typed industries, such as retail and interpersonal care.

A key reason for gender inequality in entrepreneurial businesses, according to the Kauffman compilation is "the widely held stereotype of entrepreneurship as associated largely within technology-based industries and as a male-typed or masculine activity, and the power of this stereotype to discourage women from pursuing entrepreneurship and/or detract from their ability to garner support for a new venture."

From other studies on gender bias and investing, we see an emotional disconnect between male investors and female founders, often due to the industry or product type. One woman who ran a fashion-oriented start-up told me that during a pitch session to angel investors, if she heard, "I'll ask my wife" (about whether her product proposition had market appeal), she knew it was a dead end. Other studies on gender bias have shown two other reasons for lower investment rates into women-led businesses: women tend to ask for less money than men, and women tend to be judged on performance while men are judged on potential.

Whether women's difficulty in attaining financial support for their ventures is driven by the type of businesses they start (e.g., they're not technology) or because men don't understand or care about female-focused product propositions, the problem is not necessarily solved by adding more female angels and venture capital investors into capital markets. Regardless of an investor's gender, angels and venture capitalists, by nature, are still looking for unicorns.

So, what is a woman entrepreneur to do if the cards are stacked so firmly against her business gaining traction among angel or venture capital investors? And what about all the women who never even go so far as to call themselves entrepreneur—those female entrepreneur wannabes who allow their dream to die because they found the question of financing too much of a hurdle to surmount? Women have proven themselves to be savvy, successful business managers. Does it really come down to investors' unrealistic appetites for outsized rates of return as the key deterrent to more women becoming entrepreneurs? I'm afraid it might, and here's where I'd like to make the case for why lifestyle companies can be a good investment.

Investing in lifestyle companies means investing in life. They may not be the sexy unicorns that will make you rich, but they're the businesses that keep our economy chugging along and that provide most of the jobs in this country. "Women, especially Generations X and Y, want to make their business and personal lives and aspirations work more in harmony."[20] Because of this, they often choose to limit the size of their business and not pursue outside funding from investors or loans to fuel more growth. We can theorize that the reason they choose not to pursue outside funding is because they're wary of the strings attached. As we've seen in the cases of TrueBody and Liz Lovely, those strings are all too real. Unfortunately, this possibly serves to hamstring women-led businesses and keep them unnaturally small.

What if there were other sources of capital that allowed lifestyle businesses to grow at an organic pace, and were designed for an ROI that allowed for a healthy return to investors without forcing an exit that ended in acquisition? The key, I believe, is tied up in the underlying security or structure of the investment deal. If we only think in rigid terms of debt and equity, we limit the possibilities. The business owner is either saddled with loan payments that may limit the very growth the capital is supposed to ignite, or she's headed toward selling her business (possibly sooner than she'd like) in order to give her investors an exit.

Royalty models, sometimes called *revenue-sharing models*, are a possible alternative. They defer the requirement to repay until a mutually-agreed milestone is triggered and revenue presumably has reached a level at which repayment is less of a burden. These deals also often include a safety mechanism so that if revenues (or profit) in one period fall below the target, the revenue-share payment is deferred. These models tend to be much more business-friendly while also offering investors a target rate of return with an upside potential if the company exceeds its targets. The drawback of this model is that it's really only suitable for companies that have reached a certain level of maturity and are showing steady-ish cash flow. Revenue-share models are not good for start-ups.

But this is getting too technical. Let's get back to why we should even be thinking about investing in these companies in the first place. By definition, "a lifestyle business sustains income while building the quality of life chosen by the business owner."[21] Quality of life is the key here, and a lot more value should be put on this aspect from an economic standpoint. A woman who starts a business where she can create fulfilling work for herself and others, and does so in a way that allows her to have a life beyond her business, is adding to the economic betterment of her community at the same time.

Let's compare two scenarios. Meet Cindy. She's 31, married, and has one child who's a year old. Before she went on maternity leave, she'd been working on an idea that could harness technological advances in her field to offer groundbreaking new services to her industry. She returned to work after her three-month maternity leave, but continued to work on her idea whenever she found a spare minute, which wasn't very often. Now, a year later, she's got a business plan and is ready to give it a try. She and her husband have saved and planned enough to give her a six-month runway to get the business launched and funded. She goes to a local pitch competition and wins the $25,000 prize that allows her to build a beta site and start pitching for bigger investment. It ends up taking her 10 months to get that "bigger investment" from a local incubator, but she's on her way. After year two, her investors are pressuring her to deliver on the expectations to have the company ready to shop around to bigger tech companies for acquisition. She works 10-hour days, six days a week, and is on the road a ton to sell her product as well as pitch new investors. She hardly sees her daughter, who's now almost three, and her dream of having a second child is put off until after she can sell her company. Her husband is increasingly frustrated as more of the family obligations fall to him, and he never sees his wife. The family experiences a financial drain as Cindy works for peanuts. By the end of year four, she sells her company for a hefty price, but by that time, she's brought on so much outside capital that her ownership stake is diluted down to practically nothing and while her investors walk away with seven times their original investment, she gets enough to cover the credit card debt she assumed for the company (and to support her family while not taking a salary) and not much else. She achieved the proverbial successful exit, but she's burned out, estranged from her child, and on the verge of a divorce.

Now let's consider how Cindy's life would be different if she chose to create a lifestyle company. In this scenario, Cindy negotiates a ramp-down with her employer that lets her work three days a week for six months to finish up some of her projects and train her replacement and still gives her two days a week to get her new company started. She uses some of her savings to hire a consultant to help put some structure in place and to help her find patient capital. The consultant introduces her to a group of female investors who are willing to fund her early stage needs in the form of convertible debt. This means she doesn't have to start repaying the loan right away and can put all the capital toward building the business for the next three years at which time, depending on the status of the company, she can start to repay the loan, or if the company's doing really well, the investors can choose to defer repayment one more year and then convert to a revenue-sharing model that allows Cindy to repay the investment over time at a higher rate of return than the straight loan. At the end of seven years, she's paid off her investors (who are quite happy with their 12% ROI), and she has full ownership of her company that's now grown to $3.5 million in sales and employs 14 people. She is professionally fulfilled and still has time to spend with her husband and two children.

The difference between these two scenarios demonstrates how the concentration of wealth is perpetuated. In the first scenario, Cindy's investors get a 600% return on their investment after four years, and Cindy walks away in a slightly worse financial position with personal and family issues that could lead to divorce, depression, or worse. In the second scenario, Cindy's investors get a 12% return on their investment after seven years, and Cindy has a satisfying, well-paying career with a business that creates good jobs in her community, and a happy, healthy life outside her work.

The key to making this work is finding investors who see the value of Scenario #2. Lifestyle and other long-term local businesses need more support from local community investors who invest patient capital in forms other than a traditional loan structure. This is how we create a patchwork quilt of financing to support those businesses that are built to last. I know these local community investors are out there— I've met them and helped them make investments through Milk Money— and I believe there are more who just need some encouragement and education to make the financial connections. The advent of equity crowdfunding has started the revolution, so let's take a look now at how it got started and where it's going.

I often say it all started with ice cream.

Chapter 6

Origins of Crowdfunding

In 1978, Ben & Jerry's started selling their first scoops of ice cream from a renovated gas station in downtown Burlington, Vermont. By 1984, the brand had grown so popular that the company was ready for a state-of-the-art factory to keep up with demand. The chosen site for the factory was about 30 miles southeast of Burlington, off Interstate 89, in Waterbury, Vermont.

The founders didn't limit their innovative talent solely to conjuring up wild and wonderful flavors of ice cream but applied their creativity to fundraising, too. They discovered a little known rule in the world of capital that allowed them to design a financing campaign to raise money from their friends, neighbors, and fellow Vermonters. They called the campaign "Get a Scoop of the Action." Technically speaking, it was a Vermont-only DPO, which is similar to the initial public offerings (IPOs) one hears about when a start-up goes public by selling shares on the New York Stock Exchange, NASDAQ, or other public stock exchange. The difference is that a DPO, as the *d* in its acronym indicates, is sold directly to investors, i.e., no stock exchange or stock brokers involved, and it's often limited to investors within a specific geographic region or state.

Over the course of a year, Ben & Jerry's raised over $750,000 from 1200+ Vermonters. If you do the math, that's an average investment of around $625. While many people invested more than $625, the minimum investment allowed was just $126 (in 2018 dollars that's around $300), which made it fairly affordable for average folks to become proud shareholders of their favorite local business.

A year later, in 1985, Ben Cohen and Jerry Greenfield followed their DPO by taking the company fully public through an IPO and, for the next 15 years, grew the company in accordance with its three-part mission: to make the world's best ice cream, to run a financially successful company, and to "make the world a better place."[22] Then, in 2000, Ben and Jerry discovered the hidden strings attached to being a publicly traded company. Unilever, the Anglo-Dutch consumer goods giant, came knocking on their door with a generous offer to buy the company. Generous or not, the founders did not want to sell. They feared that the huge multinational conglomerate—owner of over 400 brands such as Dove, Lever2000, and Lipton Cup-a-Soup, to name a very few—would ditch the mission and turn Ben & Jerry's into a "soulless subsidiary."[23]

Herein lies the rub. As a public corporation, the Ben & Jerry's Board of Directors arguably had a fiduciary responsibility to its shareholders to accept the highest bidder, which brings us back to Milton Friedman's quote, at the beginning of Chapter 4, that the only social responsibility of a corporation is to enhance profits for its shareholders. While the company's namesakes scrambled to cobble together a last minute counteroffer, in the end, the company was sold to the highest bidder (Unilever) for $326 million. I lived through the aftermath of the Unilever takeover during my early days at Seventh Generation, which was only a few miles from Ben & Jerry's headquarters in South Burlington, Vermont. In the early 2000s, as Unilever managers took control of its newest brand, Seventh Generation became one of the many Ben & Jerry's refugee camps to which professionals fled before being downsized or obsoleted out of a job.

Fast forward to the summer of 2009, when I found myself in a big bear-hug with Jerry Cohen at On the Rise Bakery in Richmond, Vermont. I was introduced to Jerry by Courtney Lightfoot, my first full-time employee at TrueBody, and a former executive assistant to Ben and Jerry. Courtney and I had invited Jerry to lunch to ask him about the Vermont-only stock offering because I wanted to do the same for TrueBody but with the benefit of Jerry's 20/20 hindsight and wisdom-of-the-burned to avoid the same thing happening to me. For over a year, I'd been exploring the idea of how to engage TrueBody's customers so that they would want to become its investors. I wanted to avoid the unappealing but standard practice of asking rich people for money (i.e., hitting the angel and venture capital circuit).

Jerry had some fun stories to tell about the many ways they advertised the offering (some of which, unbeknownst to them at the time, were illegal). But in the end, as my questions got more and more technical, Jerry said, "You've got to talk to Chico about this. He was the financial mastermind behind it."

A few weeks later, back at On the Rise Bakery, I was sitting across the table from Fred "Chico" Lager, who gave me the inside scoop (also the title of his memoir, published in 1994, about Ben & Jerry's). After having met affable, teddy-bear-like Jerry a few weeks earlier and having seen kooky-brilliant Ben Cohen speak on several occasions, I expected this guy would be just as quirky, especially with a name like Chico. But the first official CEO of Ben & Jerry's was a taciturn, serious-looking man with glasses and a graying mustache. When he spoke, he was quiet, direct, and somewhat understated, but I soon discovered he also had a wonderfully dry sense of humor.

During lunch, over my favorite On the Rise classic, a bagel, egg, and cheese with avocado, Chico gave me a cold hard dose of reality. "The campaign was a success in terms of raising the amount of money we'd set as a goal," he said. "But we weren't expecting the high cost of making people aware of it and managing all the paperwork after the deal closed. In the end, it got us some great PR (public relations), but in terms of logistics and cost, it might have been more hassle than it was worth."

I think he could tell that I was still determined to try it because he came back with this final blow: "And what made it work for Ben & Jerry's was that our products had national distribution and our brand was widely recognized and loved. As a start-up, you haven't yet built up the loyal following you need to really make this work."

I had to admit he was right, and, to this day, I appreciate his frankness, which probably saved me a ton of money and time. I put the idea on hold with the hope that, someday, TrueBody would be a household name that could support that kind of campaign.

Ben & Jerry's was one of the first, and certainly the best known and most successful examples of this early form of crowdfunding. Similar to the better known IPO, a DPO allows a company to raise money from anyone, regardless of whether or not they are an *accredited investor,* roughly defined as an individual with $1 million of net worth (excluding their home) and/or $200,000 of annual income. A key difference is that a DPO is often quicker and less expensive to set up since it exempts a company from having to register with the Securities and Exchange Commission (SEC). Some estimates put the legal and regulatory cost of a DPO at around $25,000, whereas an IPO can cost millions in legal expenses and filing fees. Another important difference is that DPO investors tend to have an emotional connection to the company and, therefore, take a longer-term orientation with their financial expectations, which can take the pressure off the company's management for short-term results. The DPO first became available to small businesses in 1976 and, spurred by Ben & Jerry's success plus a simplification of the rules in 1989, there was a wave of DPOs in the late 1980s and early 1990s. However, by the mid 90s, the rate dropped significantly.

Why aren't more companies doing DPOs? Chico's dose of tough love and advice to me contains the seed of the answer. There is an old saying that stocks are not bought. They are sold. This means, just as Chico pointed out, that significant effort is required to sell a company's stock. In the case of an IPO, a company hires an investment bank to make this happen. Investment bankers have existing client bases, connections, and experience in drumming up demand for their offerings. This is why they get paid the proverbial big bucks. With a DPO, the job of selling falls to the company whose management team is usually better equipped to run its business than to sell stock. Just like in the case of Ben & Jerry's, the amount of time, effort, and marketing dollars spent by a management team to sell its own offering can far outweigh the benefits of turning your loyal fan base into shareholders.

Despite all that, by the spring of 2011, I was still convinced there must be a way to achieve all the benefits of a DPO in a more cost-effective and timely manner. So I was ecstatic when I learned about a new website called ProFounder. It was started by Jessica Jackley, the founder of Kiva. Jessica's vision was to take this new concept for crowdfunding that she'd pioneered as peer-to-peer lending for women in developing countries and bring it to a new level. She knew there were women like me, here in the U.S., who needed funding just as badly as women in India, and she wanted to transform the way people invested in entrepreneurs in our country. ProFounder took the DPO concept and brought it into the 21st century using the internet to reach a much broader audience than Ben & Jerry's ever could with their "Get a Scoop of the Action" stickers on ice cream cartons.

I immediately took a deep dive into the ProFounder website and set up an account that gave me access to their campaign-planning dashboard. I had already tried a homegrown form of internet crowdfunding in 2009 with a Community Supported Enterprise (CSE) campaign, designed along the lines of Community Supported Agriculture, where people could pre-buy TrueBody Soap that would be delivered to them after I used the CSE proceeds to help pay for the production run. Similar to Community Supported Agriculture, the intent was to raise capital up front when it was needed to produce my products. Then the customers would receive their product at a later date. The concept was great—in theory—and people did subscribe to my CSE, but there was a downfall: in order to raise the amount of capital I needed, those subscribers would have had to pre-buy three years' worth of soap!

Not long after my CSE experiment, I'd learned about a new thing called Kickstarter. At first, when I checked it out, I was pretty excited. The idea of "free" money from donations was somewhat appealing, but the more I thought about it, the more I really liked the idea of having a long-term relationship with an investor versus just a donor. But not to be picky about free money, I went so far as to register on Kickstarter only to be told that my company was not "creative" enough. At that time, Kickstarter focused specifically on projects involving music, art, movies, books, etc. My consumer product business didn't fit their criteria.

So ProFounder seemed like the answer to my prayers. It was set up specifically to allow unaccredited investors to participate right alongside wealthy angel investors. It still required significant strategy and legal work because you were basically setting up a DPO in any state where you might have potential investors. To register in all 50 states would have been prohibitively expensive, so I looked at the ones where I had friends, family, and strong distribution. I remember a conference call with the ProFounder team: Jessica and cofounder Dana Muriello. It was very early in their launch, and I was one of their very first clients. They walked me through some strategic planning to maximize investor outreach and minimize legal costs.

Within about six weeks, I was far enough along with my campaign preparation to feel confident about setting a launch date in August 2011. Then one day in late July, I went to log in to my account to put the finishing touches on my campaign, typed in the URL for the ProFounder client dashboard, and nothing came up. I tried the main page and still nothing. It was as if the site didn't exist. The next day, I received an email from Jessica and Dana saying, "As you may have seen on our homepage today, we have decided to shut down ProFounder."

Actually, it was a decision forced upon them. ProFounder had run afoul of SEC and state regulators as they tried to push the envelope on this new form of crowdfunding. In August 2011, the State of California's Department of Corporations issued a formal consent order telling them to "desist and refrain" from engaging in securities transactions without being registered as a broker-dealer.[24] I was crestfallen, but in the long run, a lot of good, that affected me in ways I couldn't imagine at the time, did end up coming from their efforts. In ProFounder, one finds the seeds of today's perfectly legal Regulation Crowdfunding. In fact, after the shuttering of ProFounder, Dana spent a lot of time on Capitol Hill testifying on behalf of what would become the JOBS Act that was signed into law by President Obama in April 2012 and enacted by the SEC in May

2016. (Jessica had twins in September 2011 and was a little preoccupied during that time!)

Those few months in the spring and summer of 2011 that I spent building a campaign with ProFounder also planted a seed for my next entrepreneurial venture. In the summer of 2014, not long after my TrueBody crowdfunding experiments with CSE campaigns and ProFounder, Vermont's Department of Financial Regulation (DFR) took the pioneering step to revise the intrastate crowdfunding regulation in Vermont. Renamed the Vermont Small Business Offering (VSBO) exemption, it was the same regulation that Ben & Jerry's had used 30 years before but updated for the 21st century to allow the use of the internet and social media for Vermont-only crowdfunding campaigns.

While the VSBO was being revised and implemented at the Statehouse in Montpelier, I had recently reconnected with an old colleague who was in the very beginning stages of launching a new business. Sascha Mayer and I had met during my Seventh Generation days when her employer, JDK Design, was engaged to do some exploratory brand work. Sascha and I spent a lot of time on the road doing focus groups, and we bonded over the fact that we were both pregnant at the same time.

By 2014, when Sascha and I reconnected, our babies were eight years old, and I'd launched and managed two start-ups. Sascha was still working full-time at JDK, but she was also taking steps toward becoming an entrepreneur herself. Through the incredible foresight, wisdom, and creativity of her manager, Michael Jager (the "J" in JDK), she and a fellow JDK colleague, Christine Dodson, had been encouraged to incubate their entrepreneurial vision within JDK. This vision had recently become Mamava, a company devoted to creating lactation solutions for moms on the go. Sascha and Christine had three prototypes placed in and around Burlington, Vermont, most notably (and publicly) at Burlington International Airport. Early response was positive, and they were ready to officially launch the company with a vision to roll out their lactation suites to airports, workplaces, schools, and other venues across the country. They brought me on as the first member of their launch team, and for a long time, it was just me wearing multiple hats as befits an entrepreneur, but I was mainly focused on operations and finance. Eventually, Sascha negotiated a step-down in duties with JDK to be able to work part-time on Mamava; Christine remained full-time at JDK and was our sounding board and advisor.

If you've never seen a Mamava unit (now in over 1,000 locations around the U.S. and beyond), they are about the size of one of those old photo booths you might see at the mall. In other words, they are not small. However, they are impeccably designed to be welcoming, comfortable, and eye-catching (designed purposefully to resemble a breast!), and thus, they are not inexpensive to build. My point here is that my first order of business was to figure out where to find the capital to build some inventory and launch the business. Like most start-ups, Mamava got its early funding from founders, family, and friends. But it would need more money, a lot more, to really get the ball rolling.

My first and biggest project was to define and recommend a financing strategy for Sascha and Christine. I had a whole lot of firsthand experience raising money for TrueBody that was directly relevant to Mamava's situation. I also had some strong opinions on what worked and what didn't, especially for women running a consumer-facing (i.e., not technology) company. I continued to believe in the potential of crowdfunding, which Kickstarter and Indiegogo were now starting to prove with successful donation-based campaigns. The serendipitous timing of the VSBO regulatory changes in June 2014 opened the door for Vermont to become one of the first states in the country to adopt intrastate crowdfunding regulations that made it fairly easy for anyone (not just the wealthy) to invest directly in Vermont-based companies. As soon as I learned about VSBO, I started laying the groundwork for a Mamava crowdfunding campaign. Sascha loved the idea of appealing to the many friends, neighbors, business acquaintances—all moms—who'd expressed moral support for Mamava and now might provide financial support.

By early fall 2014, I'd written the plan for a web-based platform and marketing outreach program to engage Vermont investors. Through all of the fundraising I'd done with TrueBody, I had a basic idea of the legal needs for such a campaign and, more importantly, what questions still needed answers to complete the plan. The next step was to meet with Mamava's attorney, Eli Moulton, to get answers and his feedback on the plan. Eli and I went way back. He'd been my attorney with TrueBody. He helped me navigate its traditional fundraising campaigns, he had endured many conversations where I probed the legal boundaries on how to include unaccredited investors, and he advised on my early crowdfunding attempts through my CSE campaigns. He also played a pivotal role in the regulatory changes that led to the VSBO exemption in June 2014 by testifying at the Vermont Statehouse in favor of the revisions. I like to believe that all those hours of meetings where I was surely a pain in Eli's neck asking, "but what if…," a thousand times as I pushed the legal envelope for TrueBody played some role in encouraging Eli's testimony in favor of VSBO. My squeaky wheel finally got some grease!

On a crisp October morning, I walked into Eli's familiar office with Sascha. The sunlight that filtered through colorful fall foliage added to my optimism and excitement as I set out to put VSBO into action. After I laid out the goal and details of the plan, Eli started listing the areas where we'd need his help—things like drafting and finalizing the offering documents, verifying that all potential investors were Vermont residents, tracking and managing investor details, and fielding their questions over the life of the investment. He ballparked the cost at around $6,000, after which I watched the enthusiasm drain from Sascha's face. I knew right then that she didn't have the appetite —and Mamava didn't have the budget—to launch a crowdfunding campaign. As Mamava's Chief Financial Officer (CFO), I said as much before we left the meeting. But as we walked out of Eli's office, I asked Sascha not to give up on the concept just yet. This meeting had jolted some wheels into motion in my mind. As I got in my car to drive back to my office, I took off my Mamava CFO hat, put on my entrepreneur hat, and called Louisa Schibli.

Louisa and I had met a few years before when I was running one of my early crowdfunding experiments with TrueBody. The novelty of my CSE campaign had inspired a big article on the cover of the "Business Monday" section of the *Burlington Free Press*. Louisa was so intrigued by the article she called me out of the blue for an interview for her blog, *MoogleVermont*. We did the phone interview and then decided to meet for coffee a few weeks later. At that meeting, we talked for hours, realizing we had a lot in common: we're the same age, we're both moms (although her kids are 5–10 years older than mine), and we both had a strong commitment to the entrepreneurial ecosystem in Vermont. We continued to meet periodically, especially after I shut down TrueBody, always on the topic of what was missing for entrepreneurs and how we might be able to help. We brainstormed a bunch of different ideas for what this could look like, and even started bouncing some of our concepts off a beloved business advisor at the Vermont Small Business Development Center. We knew in our guts that someday we'd find a way to go into business together. As I drove away from the Mamava meeting that fateful fall day in 2014, my first words to Louisa when she answered the phone were, "I've found it. I know how we're going to work together."

Within a few months, we had a registered business entity, a logo, and a business plan for Milk Money. It would become the online platform, technical assistance provider, marketing outreach augmenter, and investor relations manager for companies that wanted to raise capital from fellow Vermonters but that didn't have the time, budget, or know-how to do it themselves. Louisa and I were a perfect match to make this happen. I brought the entrepreneurial, business management, and, especially, the capital raising experience; she was the web design, user experience, and social media expert. While she found and managed a freelance website creator to build the site, I worked my networks in the finance and entrepreneurial support world within Vermont to lay the groundwork for our entrepreneur outreach and investor awareness and education campaigns.

We bootstrapped most of the initial launch costs ourselves and received a small but timely (and greatly appreciated) loan from a friend of Louisa's who is a pioneer of women investing in women. This got the site ready for its beta launch in early July of 2015. Through some serendipitous timing, I was introduced to Rob Miller, CEO of Vermont State Employees Credit Union (VSECU), and we met the day after Louisa and I had soft-launched the site. As Rob and I sat in a coffeeshop in Burlington on a beautiful summer morning, it was great to be able to illustrate our plans for Milk Money by showing off parts of the new site. After I gave him the spiel, Rob gave me a pointed look and asked, "How are you financing this? Do you need money to launch? Because I believe my organization might be interested in investing."

I didn't literally fall out of my chair, but the stunned look on my face, with mouth agape, was just as embarrassing. By the way, for all you aspiring entrepreneurs out there, let me say this: in my experience, something like this rarely happens! When I finally regained my wits, I responded, "We've been bootstrapping so far and have planned a slow rollout over time in accordance with our budget. But additional funding would allow us to ramp up much more quickly and effectively. Are you serious about this?"

Turns out he was serious. His board and management team, however, took a little more time and encouragement to jump on the bandwagon. This was brand new territory for a 70+ year old bank-like institution that was used to making loans, not investments. There's a big difference between the two. Loans come with collateral and well-defined interest rates and repayment plans. An investment implies an equity arrangement, which simply means ownership, usually in the form of stock. Unlike the well-defined repayment plan of debt, the financial gain from an equity investment is undefined and uncertain. Traditionally, financial gain from an equity investment comes when a business is sold to a bigger company for a stock price that is (hopefully) much higher than what you paid for it. We spent many hours in long discussions with Rob's team answering (and re-answering) a double-barreled question: "So how much will we make from this investment and when will we get it?"

See, the thing with an equity investment is you just don't know. So why would anyone want to make an equity investment, you might ask. Well, by the very nature of its payout being undefined and uncertain, it brings unlimited potential for gain. This is the allure of equity; who hasn't wished they'd been an early investor in Amazon, Google, Facebook, or Ben & Jerry's and cashed out with a big payday when they went public? This is what drives angel investors and venture capital funds: the enticing hunt for the next "unicorn." But it's not necessarily what was driving a credit union like VSECU. They stated, emphatically and often, that they weren't looking to make a huge profit on this investment and were doing it as much to support the business community as for their own financial gain. And this is probably why they kept defaulting to the structure of a loan for the investment (in addition to the fact that loans were all they knew how to do). It was up to us to educate them on why a loan is usually not the best way to finance an early stage company, and, in fact, can often be a recipe for premature death due to what I call the killer C's: collateral and cash flow.

Most loan agreements from banks and credit unions require collateral. Think of collateral as a pledge of property that could be sold to pay off a loan if you're otherwise unable to make the payments. If you've ever gotten a car loan or mortgage, your collateral is the car or home that you're buying, which means that if you can't make the loan payments, the bank has the right to take your car or home and sell it to repay the debt.

So now, let's think about collateral as it relates to a start-up business looking for a loan. Most start-ups don't own real estate or other property to put up as collateral, especially not a web-based company like Milk Money, where the company's main assets were its website and our expertise, networks, and experience. In cases like this, the owners of the company are usually required to pledge personal property as collateral for a business loan. I was required to do this with TrueBody when I pledged my home as collateral for a business loan through Community Capital of Vermont. After

TrueBody, I promised myself (and my husband) we'd never do this again, and Louisa was of no mind to put her house up as collateral either, so that stalled the discussion of a loan pretty quickly.

But it wasn't just the collateral requirement that made a loan inappropriate for Milk Money at this stage. More importantly, it was the repayment structure. Companies that are just getting up and running usually don't have a lot of cash coming in from sales yet. They're still building the foundations of the business and working to get some initial sales that will build a reputation that leads to more new sales and ideally drive repeat business. This all takes time, and it takes money to be able to pay the bills to literally keep the lights on while you're building your business. Just like a newborn baby, an early stage company takes a lot of care and nurturing to keep it alive, healthy, and growing to the point where it can walk on its own. So, to add the burden of a loan payment at this time could drain precious cash away from its use in building the business.

Conversely, an equity investment gives a company a little breathing room to focus efforts (and cash) on building the business in the early years and pushes the repayment responsibility out to a time when the company is successful and better able to share its profitability with those early investors who believed in it. Now, of course, this breathing room means those investors have to be patient as they wait to see what happens with the business. This waiting makes equity investments more risky than debt because there is always the possibility a company may fail before an equity investor ever sees a dime. Theoretically, even if a company fails, a lender stands to get at least some of its money back, whereas an equity investor loses everything. This is why equity investors expect to make a bigger gain on their investment than they'd get from a typical loan.

Back to the Milk Money/VSECU example. As I mentioned above, VSECU stated, emphatically and often, that it wasn't making this investment for the financial gain; it was doing it for the opportunities that Milk Money would create for its members and the community in the form of increased entrepreneurial activity, job creation, and the circulation of wealth within Vermont's local economy. But when all was said and done, the VSECU team did expect some return—this wasn't a charitable donation—and their inability to truly detach from debt-like expectations became apparent much later.

However, in late 2015, Louisa and I believed we'd effectively convinced the VSECU team of the benefits of ownership in Milk Money; papers were signed and money deposited in Milk Money's account. The official launch was set for February 10, 2016 to coincide with VSECU's major rebranding campaign. A big media event was staged at the main VSECU branch in Montpelier. Several local TV stations, newspapers, and reporters from Vermont Public Radio were there. The event was a beautiful example of a value-added investor. In addition to their cash investment, VSECU invested its significant marketing muscle. It orchestrated a powerful public launch for the Milk Money website and continued these efforts over the next few years by featuring Milk Money in its member newsletters, by writing blog posts to encourage local investment, and through other social media outreach efforts to spread the word about Milk Money.

Once the site was officially launched, the real work began in earnest. We knew the concept would appeal to business owners and entrepreneurs because, quite frankly, entrepreneurs always need money and we were providing an innovative new way to try to get it. I used to joke, "We've got Money in our name–entrepreneurs will find us." And find us they did.

Over the course of two years, Louisa and I met with over 120 entrepreneurs, which prompted us, early on, to develop a screening tool to evaluate the viability of their potential offering. Our Milk Money Readiness Assessment was a service to investors as the first level of due diligence that screened out candidates whose business plan was incomplete or otherwise not a good fit for a VSBO campaign. It was also a useful feedback tool for entrepreneurs as we provided guidance and suggestions on how to improve their readiness capabilities. For Milk Money, it was just smart business. We knew we needed to come out of the gates strong with a couple successful campaigns to prove this newfangled crowd-investing concept would work. The Readiness Assessment helped us find those companies with the most potential for success.

Not only did Milk Money need to prove the concept to our own investment partner (VSECU) and the rest of the Vermont financial scene, I needed a little proof myself. As an entrepreneur who'd been researching and experimenting with crowdfunding concepts for a pretty long time, I had a healthy dose of confidence in our proposition, but there was still that little voice in the back of my mind that said, "Yeah, but will anyone actually write a check?" Would anyone else see the power of what we'd created to engage community members in their own economic future?

Now that we built it, would investors come?

Chapter 7

The Future of Crowdfunding

Did people make investments through Milk Money? Yes. During the period of 2016 through early 2018, Milk Money launched nine campaigns that raised nearly $370,000 from 115 Vermonters. That's an average investment of roughly $3,200, but the median investment amount was closer to $1,200. While several (mostly accredited) investors wrote checks for $5,000–$10,000, we had plenty that came in at the minimum of $250.

It started to feel like Milk Money was delivering on its vision to engage the Main Street investor alongside those who qualified as angel investors. Not only that, Milk Money was helping business owners reach people beyond their F&F investor network. One of my favorite examples of this came when one of our earliest campaign companies received its first investment from a *new friend* (I like this term better than *stranger*). The company was Vermont Evaporator Company and the a-ha moment came during part of the investment process managed by Milk Money that required us to get the business owner's signature on any new investment document. It was a laborious process to track down track down busy entrepreneurs and get them to sign paperwork, but if they wanted their money, they had to sign the papers. However, through this process, the entrepreneurs not only got their investment money, they also became aware of each new investor, which was exactly the kind of relationship-building that Milk Money was designed to facilitate.

Kate McCabe, an attorney-turned-entrepreneur and CEO of Vermont Evaporator Company, was a neophyte in the world of raising start-up capital. The plain vanilla name of her company belies her folksy yet brilliant brand proposition. It all started when Kate, her husband and cofounder, Justin, and their two kids decided to try their hand at tapping 25 maple trees in the backyard of their Montpelier home to make their own maple syrup. A little known fact (outside maple country) is that it takes roughly 40 gallons of sap to yield one gallon of maple syrup, which you get by boiling the sap for several hours (and often days). Some small-scale DIY sugarmakers boil sap in their kitchen, which can make a mess when the sugary steam that evaporates from your pot creates a sticky coating on your ceiling. More often, it's boiled outside in a pan set on a gas grill. Kate and Justin opted for the outdoor setup, complete with Thanksgiving turkey broiling pan and propane grill, and their first attempt as sugarmakers ended in disappointment after they realized they'd spent as much or more on propane as they would have if they'd just bought syrup from their local food co-op.

Undeterred, the McCabes searched everywhere for a backyard-scale sap evaporator, but all they found were industrial size evaporators that cost thousands of dollars and were designed for commercial-scale sugaring operations that build sugar shacks to house the whole operation. Justin, an engineer and patent attorney, knew there had to be a better way. Tinkering away over the summer and fall before the next sugaring season (roughly late February through early April, depending on the weather), he created the Sapling, a backyard sap evaporator perfect for beginners and hobbyists. And he didn't make just one: he built a dozen in the family garage and posted an ad for them on Craig's List. Within two weeks, every Sapling (priced around $700) was sold. That's when Kate-the-attorney became Kate-the-entrepreneur, and she soon found her way to Milk Money to raise capital to get the new company launched.

Kate did a fantastic job of preselling her investment opportunity to her large network of family and friends in and around Montpelier. When her campaign was officially launched, she immediately got a flood of investments from enthusiastic (and familiar) supporters. A couple weeks into her campaign, as we took her through the latest batch of investment documents to sign, Kate came across one name she did not recognize and this stopped her cold. Someone she did not know thought highly enough of her business proposition to make an investment of $250. The check size didn't matter. It was the sense of validation that gave her a huge boost of confidence. And then something even more beautiful happened. It dawned on Kate that she was now responsible for someone else's money and responsible for managing the expectations that came along with it. This feeling is one of the most powerful by-products of local investment: The sense of accountability that encourages business owners to make thoughtful and appropriate use of the funding provided by their community. It is how we start to build more resilient, sustainable communities of engaged citizen investors and responsible business owners. And it is why I love the concept of crowdfunding.

We still have some work to do to get it right, though. By late 2017, just as Louisa and I were starting to feel that we'd proved the crowdfunding concept was working and were ironing out the kinks in Milk Money's business model, momentum began to slow. For the previous two years, we hadn't needed to do much outreach to entrepreneurs because they were finding us faster than we could get to all of them. But now the pipeline started to dry up. Why?

For one thing, although we'd put most of our education and outreach efforts into attracting investors—and that was clearly working—it was not working fast or big enough. It still took a lot of work on the entrepreneur's side to maintain a consistent social media campaign to attract enough attention from potential investors to reach their target. Milk Money did as much as it was legally allowed to do to promote campaigns through our own social media, but the real effort had to come from the business doing the raise. We worked with a local marketing firm to design a very affordable Milk Money package of social media consulting and support so that our campaign companies could get a little expert guidance (plus some additional hands on deck) to promote their campaigns. Unfortunately, not one of our campaign companies signed up. Even at the special negotiated rate, most of them said they just couldn't afford it. Truth be told, they could barely afford Milk Money's fee. We had begun to uncover the paradox that was to haunt us in coming months: the businesses that needed Milk Money's help the most to raise money to grow their business did not have the money to pay for our help.

Was this a design flaw in Milk Money's business model? Maybe. When Louisa and I first discussed how we wanted to structure our business, we considered creating Milk Money as a nonprofit or even as a cooperative, but in the end, we set it up as a for-profit company largely because we believed that clients would take their campaigns more seriously, i.e., put more effort into them, if they had to pay for the services we provided. The key question then was how much to charge them and when.

The when part was largely decided for us by law. Unlike donation-based crowdfunding sites like Kickstarter and Indiegogo that take their fee as a percentage of the amount raised at the end of a campaign, equity crowdfunding sites like Milk Money were prohibited by law to take this kind of success fee unless they became a registered broker-dealer. A *broker-dealer* is defined as a person or firm in the business of buying and selling securities for its own account or on behalf of its customers.[25] Since Milk Money and other state-based equity crowdfunding platforms neither bought nor sold securities—they simply created a meeting place for investors and entrepreneurs and facilitated the transaction between the two parties—there was no need for these platforms to go through the long and extremely expensive process of registering as a broker-dealer.

Milk Money's revenue model was set up like a consulting fee based on the number of hours we estimated it would take us to prepare, launch, and maintain a campaign. At first, we were told by the Vermont DFR that we had to charge our fee and receive payment of that fee before a campaign was ever launched so that it in no way resembled a success fee, i.e., it couldn't look like the fee was being paid from the proceeds of the campaign. Over time, and with much negotiation with the DFR, we were able to modify the payment structure to allow entrepreneurs to pay our fee over time (as funds came in from the campaign) so long as the amount was stated and agreed upon before the campaign launched, and it also had to be very clear that the fee was required to be paid whether or not the campaign reached its goal.

This change made it somewhat easier for campaign companies to pay Milk Money's fees, but the pipeline dried up nonetheless. To this day, there continues to be only a slight trickle of interest from entrepreneurs, and Milk Money has not posted a new campaign since January 2018. In October 2018, Milk Money merged with Vermont Innovation Commons, an accelerator project in Burlington's New North End that was still under construction when this book went to print, and Louisa, Milk Money's cofounder, joined its parent company, Vermont Works Management Company, where she continues to explore options to improve Milk Money's business model.

One of these options may be to eschew the state-based focus of the platform and take advantage of opportunities opened by Regulation Crowdfunding at the national level. Following the enactment of national crowdfunding regulations under Title III of the JOBS Act in 2016, crowdfunding platforms now have the option of registering as a "funding portal" rather than having to go through the full process to become a registered broker-dealer.[26] Becoming a registered funding portal is somewhat less laborious and costly than registering as a broker-dealer, and it does allow a platform to get paid a percentage of the proceeds from a successful campaign. Could this be a viable option for Milk Money?

Possibly, but I believe there are bigger, more systemic issues than a platform's revenue model at work, and they're not limited to Milk Money or Vermont. For another piece of evidence, we can look to the state-based crowdfunding platform, Hatch Oregon, that launched in January 2015. Louisa and I were introduced to Amy Pearl, the founder of Hatch Oregon in the fall of 2015, not long after our own beta site was launched. By the time we officially launched Milk Money in February 2016, we had spent many hours on the phone with Amy sharing stories and comparing notes. Our two state-based platforms on either side of the country were pioneers in crowdfunding as they took bold steps to introduce citizens to local investment opportunities well before the national crowdfunding regulations finally came into being.

Hatch Oregon's platform is conceptually the same as Milk Money's with a few notable differences. For one thing, Hatch Oregon is structured as a nonprofit. Another significant difference between the two is the level of service provided by the platforms. On the one hand, Milk Money charged a fee ranging between $2,500–$5,000 to create a client company's campaign that included preparation of customized offering documents and marketing materials plus shepherding all of these materials through the acceptance process with Vermont's DFR. On the other, Hatch Oregon put entrepreneurs through an eight-week cohort-based Accelerator program in which a group of entrepreneurs was taught how to create offering documents and marketing materials that they then had to produce, submit for regulatory compliance, and distribute themselves. Cost to participate in the Accelerator cohort was $3,000.

Over its first two years, Hatch Oregon helped 15 companies raise over $440,000 from more than 400 Oregonians. But then, it started to experience a drop-off in interest from businesses, just as Milk Money did. Today the Hatch Oregon site is somewhat static with a disclaimer across the top that says, "We are updating our material to reflect the new rules updated on January 1, 2018." Like Milk Money, Hatch Oregon has also recently experienced a significant change in leadership, staff, and board membership. The fate of each platform remains to be seen.

So what's going on here? Did these early pioneers of state-based equity crowdfunding simply become irrelevant after the national crowdfunding regulations were enacted in 2016? Certainly, the allure of being able to reach beyond a state's borders to attract many more millions of possible investors is very compelling, despite the fact that many of the state crowdfunding regulations are far more generous than the national rule. (For example, several states allow unaccredited individuals to invest up to $5,000 or even $10,000, whereas the national limit is just $2,200 per unaccredited investor.) But even on the national level, with the potential to reach millions of investors, crowdfunding results have been only modestly encouraging. It's been over three years since the enactment of the national crowdfunding rule and while recent data show 144% growth in the number of unique offerings from 2017–2018 and a 190% increase in the total number of investors in successful offerings over the same period, the absolute numbers tell a different story.[27]

The statistics in the previous sentence were drawn from the January 2019 report prepared by Crowdfund Capital Advisors for the SEC, titled *The 2018 State of Regulation Crowdfunding*, and this same report shows the total number of investors in successful offerings in 2018 was 147,448. In other words, fewer than 150,000 Americans participated in U.S. securities-based crowdfunding under Title III of the JOBS Act. That's about 0.07% of the adult population in the U.S. The report goes on to point out that after three years, the market has yet to move beyond infancy stage; the authors are "still waiting for the inflection point at which issuers, investors and dollars will grow exponentially." I can't help but wonder (to paraphrase Carrie Bradshaw in *Sex and the City*): is equity crowdfunding just a passing fad?

There have been plenty of news articles and blog posts written in 2018 and early 2019 that echo this question with titles like "Why Equity Crowdfunding is Not Living Up to the Hype."[28] A common theory is the need for more education to build awareness and to generate enthusiasm for the concept among potential investors. This is an opinion I wholeheartedly share.

Almost six months before we launched the first Milk Money campaign on our platform, Louisa and I started an Invest Local education series to help people become aware of this new opportunity and to generate interest in the concept in general. The education series consisted mostly of evening events held at restaurants, universities, local businesses, and branches of VSECU all around the state. For the most part, turnout was promising (except one particularly cold, snowy evening in mid-January in Burlington, Vermont's largest city) and enthusiastic. The interest was genuine, and the questions were instructive as they helped us understand the kinds of information people would need to take concrete steps toward investment. We used the experience to tailor the website, write an e-book (*Invest Local: A Beginner's Guide for the Thoughtful Investor*), and improve the educational events to help get the general public ready to make investments as we prepared to launch the first campaigns.

By the way, Louisa and I can't take credit for coming up with the idea for this Invest Local series. It's an idea we borrowed from our friends at Hatch Oregon who were hitting the highways and byways of Oregon while we were still testing our beta site in 2015. We also can't complain about all the late night drives home from events around the state. Our longest excursion was a six-hour round trip to Bennington, a town in the southwest corner of Vermont that borders New York state. That was nothing compared with the stories we heard from the Hatch crew about frequent 10+ hour round-trip adventures to the far-flung regions of Oregon. We told ourselves many times we're lucky Vermont is a small state.

All joking aside, even in the small state of Vermont, we had only just begun to scratch the surface on the amount of education that is still needed to bring this nascent invest local concept into the mainstream. But I think it's more than the need for more investor education that is keeping equity crowdfunding from reaching its full potential. All the education in the world will not change the fact that in order for an individual to make an informed decision on a direct, local investment—especially for a smallish dollar amount of $500-$1000— still requires a lot of time and effort. For the wise investor, the process of researching investment opportunities, often called *doing your due diligence*, takes hours of poring over campaign materials, reading offering documents, evaluating financial statements, and determining if an offering is a good fit with your portfolio. Maybe if you know the entrepreneur and are making an investment as an act of moral support (akin to F&F investing), it might be an easier decision. But if we want to move a significant portion of our savings and investment dollars into community-based investments, we are signing ourselves up for a lot of homework under the current crowdfunding setup.

This is why I believe equity crowdfunding could run the risk of becoming just another fad. It's fun at first because it's new and exciting, but, over the long-term, it's just too much work. Before we risk throwing the baby out with the bathwater, though, let's do like any good entrepreneur would do and look for the *pivot*— a strategic reorientation or reimagining of the original vision. Crowdfunding as a concept is on the right track. We just need to determine what can be tweaked to keep the best parts of the concept moving forward and improve on whatever is not working.

As I watched Milk Money's pipeline run dry, my entrepreneurial intuition pointed me toward this pivot: find a way for investors to pool both their money and their due diligence efforts and invest together. I'm talking about a fund, a community investment fund to be exact. Not only could it lessen the due diligence burden by sharing the work across a group of people (or even a professional manager), at the same time, it could reduce risk by spreading the pool of dollars over more investments, much like a mutual fund does. In finance-speak, that's called diversifying your portfolio, which is something any financial advisor will tell you is a good thing to do.

Sounds logical, right? So logical that you might wonder why no one is doing it. In fact, some regions and communities already have a version of a community investment fund in the form of community development loan funds. These loan funds are administered by CDFIs and are required to have a stated mission about creating economic opportunity for small businesses or individuals, which means they put "creating economic opportunity" above shareholder return.[29]

So community development loan funds, by definition, are in the business of generating social ROI alongside financial ROI. Even though they tend to charge higher interest rates than banks and other traditional lenders in order to offset the additional risk of their loans, they at least take that risk where others fear to tread. Their mission-driven lending philosophies incorporate the greater community good of creating jobs and supporting business growth in specific industries such as child-care, affordable housing, and local food system development. In fact, many community development loan funds—and industry partners like the CDFI Fund, the Opportunity Finance Network, and the Urban Institute—regularly report statistics on the number of small businesses started, jobs created, affordable housing built, community facilities expanded, and quality education supported by their lending activities. Community development loan funds realize that part of their return will come in the form of a more vibrant and resilient local economy.

Yet despite all the good work of community development loan funds, they are not a be-all-end-all solution, and they have their limitations. For one thing, many CDFIs do not allow individuals to invest in their loan funds, and of those that do, only a mere fraction allow unaccredited individuals to invest. Traditionally, community development loan funds have secured most, if not all, of the funding for their charitable loan work from grants and low-interest loans from philanthropic foundations, the U.S. government, and banks. More are starting to allow investment from individuals, but then only from accredited individuals. Still, there are a few praiseworthy standouts such as the New Hampshire Community Loan Fund, Vermont Community Loan Fund, Pioneer Valley Grows Fund, Northern California Community Loan fund, the Boston Impact Initiative, and others that allow investment from anyone, regardless of wealth status. The CDFI locator tool at ofn.org is a great resource for finding a CDFI in your region, and these community development loan funds remain a great place to invest some of your savings or retirement funds. But we need more of them, and we really need new options to increase community support for local economic development.

Another more obvious limitation of CDFIs is their focus on debt financing, which, as we saw in the case of Liz Lovely, is not always the best answer when a business needs money to grow. Liz Lovely received significant debt funding in its early days, so much that it eventually maxed out the amount that lenders (even CDFIs) were willing to lend—a company's cash flow can only support so much debt repayment, after all. In such a situation, many businesses start to think about offering up equity as a better option to attract growth capital. Equity postpones the need for paying a return to investors until some point in the future thus giving business owners a little breathing room to reinvest short-term profits into growing their business.

Unfortunately for Liz Lovely and other lifestyle business owners (who tend to be women), their "built to last" businesses with a track record of steady (versus meteoric hockey stick) growth are just not attractive to the main source of equity capital: angel and venture capital investors. So if these businesses have maxed out and/or decided against debt financing options, and if traditional equity sources are uninterested in their offering, what is left for them? Many suffer the fate of Liz Lovely and TrueBody and shut down their businesses because they can't access the capital they need to grow to a sustainable level. This is where new types of community investment funds plus near-equity investment structures are needed to fill the gap.

Let's start with near-equity investment structures. The most common forms of near-equity are *convertible notes* and *royalty agreements*. Both are structured similarly to a loan but with important, differentiating features that make them friendlier and more patient forms of capital for entrepreneurs and, at the same time, make them attractive investment opportunities for investors.

Convertible notes are set up like a loan with a defined interest rate and payback period but with two key differences:

1. Convertible notes typically include a grace period of anywhere between three to seven years during which no loan payments are made.
2. The end of the grace period triggers a conversion opportunity: either the company starts repaying the loan OR it converts the investment into shares of stock or a royalty agreement (more on royalty agreements below).

A key benefit of convertible notes for entrepreneurs is that it postpones the burden of loan payments until a time when, theoretically, a company is better established and has sufficient cash flow to repay the debt. It also gives investors the opportunity to participate in a company's success if it exceeds expectations, by giving them the upside potential of equity or a higher payout under a royalty agreement.

Like convertible notes, royalty agreements are similar to a loan in that they involve a structured repayment of the original investment plus a rate of return, and there is a defined end point when the investment is repaid and the investment relationship is concluded. Often, royalty agreements are set up as a revenue share model wherein a company pays its investors a percentage of revenue once it has achieved certain milestones, such as twelve consecutive months of profitable operations. The total payout of an investment is capped as a percentage of the original investment. For example, once an investor has been repaid her original investment amount plus 7.5%, the royalty agreement is satisfied, and the investment relationship ends. The risk/reward for the investor (and the company, for that matter) lies in how long it takes to satisfy the royalty agreement. For a profitable company with steadily growing revenue, the repayment period will go fast, as it takes fewer royalty payments to reach the investment cap. A company with slower revenue growth or inconsistent profitability may see a longer payback period, as smaller royalty payments take time to accumulate up to the investment cap.[*]

In addition to the benefits listed above, near-equity investment structures are particularly well-suited to support long-term economic development. Unlike equity, they offer a way for investors to get a return on their investment without a company having to sell out. Said another way, these investment structures encourage companies to focus on sustainable growth and profitability while enabling them to put down roots within a community. For this reason, they are an ideal structure for community investment funds that want to be more than just another loan fund.

---

[*] These are simplified explanations of convertible notes and royalty agreements, both of which can include lots of bells & whistles that confer additional benefit and/or control to either the issuing company or the investor. But the general gist is accurate.

A pivot toward community investment funds is starting to happen but is still very much in its infancy. Unfortunately, the creation of community investment funds is not an easy thing to accomplish because of a federal securities law called the Investment Company Act of 1940. This is the law that governs the creation of mutual funds, hedge funds, and yes, community investment funds, and it imposes a heavy compliance burden unless you can find an acceptable exemption from the 1940 Act. Until recently, very few have tried to find innovative ways to work around the 1940 Act with an exemption, but I'm happy to report that there is some pioneering work being done by organizations like the Boston Ujima Project, the Northeast Kingdom (NEK) Prosperity Fund, and a few others, and this work is now driving momentum toward creative community investing solutions. These groups are creating funds to pool money from individuals, regardless of wealth status, in order to make near-equity investments into community businesses. The Boston Ujima Project also has the added bonus of incorporating democratic governance into its fund, which means it'll give investors a say in how their money is invested.

How does a community investment fund work? What would democratic governance look like? To find these answers, let's return now to our budding entrepreneur, Beth Tudor, for the second part of "Future Capital" and see how things work out for her.

It's a fictional story, of course, but someday soon, something like it can and will happen.

Chapter 8

Future Capital Part II

When last we left Beth, her business plan had been accepted for the Moreland Community Fund's Pitch Day and she was realizing that before going public with her plans, she might want to let her current boss know what she was up to. As she sat in the familiar chair across the desk from John Holland, her long-time manager and mentor at Holland & Sons, she took a deep breath, looked him straight in the eye, and then launched into her well-rehearsed speech.

"John, I want to start by saying how much I appreciate all I've learned at Holland & Sons over the years as I worked my way up through the company. You've built a great team, and I've loved being part of it, but . . . I'm ready for a change. On nights and weekends, I've been working on a business plan for a new way to use technology to support a distribution system that's based on a cooperative business model. It takes the best of what I've learned here without being competitive with Holland, and I'm ready to try my hand at running my own company. But don't worry! I'm not going to jump ship right away. I'd like to propose a transition period where I stay on and help you promote or hire my replacement, so I can train them and make the transition as seamless as possible for you. Maybe over 6–12 weeks? What do you think?"

John's facial expression started as mild shock but slowly softened into a smile. "Well, I can't say I'm surprised. You've always been such a go-getter, and, lately, I've noticed that you've been quieter and more complacent in team meetings. I figured you were just getting comfortable with the prospect of leveling out in your position. I realize there's not much room for growth here beyond where you are now. This seems like a big step though . . ." She could tell he was letting all of what she'd said sink in before going further. This was one of the qualities she'd come to respect about John, and she knew her best response was no response, to just keep quiet and let him process.

It didn't take long before John lifted his eyes from his desk and said, "I hear you when you say that what you're proposing won't be competitive with Holland but . . . would you mind telling me a little more about your idea or even sharing your business plan?" Beth was both pleased and a little worried about sharing her business plan. Even though her idea was not directly in line with Holland's current business model, who's to say they couldn't try to add it as a subsidiary? With their good reputation and relationship with banks, they could probably get the money in a heartbeat to get it started. But then she remembered that a key part of her plan was to build her business as a cooperative that would be owned by the manufacturers who needed distribution but didn't have the capacity to build a distribution system themselves. This characteristic is what made her plan particularly unique and gave her a competitive advantage. As these thoughts ran their course, she also remembered that her business advisor, Stephanie, had given her a standard Non-Disclosure Agreement (NDA) to use with anyone who wanted to read her business plan, in order to preserve confidentiality.

With a little hesitation and a sheepish look on her face, she replied, "Well, first I should tell you that I've been working with an advisor over at the Small Business Development Center, and she was pretty firm in recommending that I have people sign an NDA before I go into too much detail. It's not that I don't trust you, but it does seem like a good idea—for both of our sakes." A light of respect shone in John's eye as he agreed to sign and commented that an NDA was a smart business practice.

Breathing a sigh of relief, she talked John through the general ideas of her business plan. He soon came to see that Beth's idea was, indeed, not competitive, and he said as much. "If we wanted to do something like this within Holland, it would have to be as a subsidiary with its own separate team. We just don't have the capacity for something like that. Nor do I think it's in the best long-term interest of the company. I think you're on to something good here, and I wish you well with it. I also appreciate your willingness to give us time to transition properly. Let's talk about those details now."

In the end, Beth and John negotiated an 8-week transition period during which they planned to promote one of Beth's direct reports into her position. At the end of the conversation, she happily gave him a copy of her business plan, knowing that she could look forward to his continued input as a fellow entrepreneur and mentor. Having John on her side felt really good.

The morning of the MCF pitch presentation dawned clear and bright, but Beth was feeling anything but clear or bright after waking up at 4 a.m. with her presentation scrolling incessantly through her mind. After a morning run with Baji and several cups of coffee, she dressed in the most formal business attire she owned (after seven years of business casual), and headed to the local university, which had donated use of its main auditorium for the event.

She was welcomed at the door by Jed, the MCF Portfolio Manager, whom she hadn't seen since her initial meeting with him seven weeks earlier. Since that first meeting, Beth had learned from her business advisor that Jed had left a high-paying job as an investment banker in New York about eight years ago to move home and take care of his aging parents. He'd since married and had two young children, and in addition to his role with the MCF, he was an adjunct professor of finance at the university.

Jed welcomed her in, gave her a preprinted nametag, and confirmed that her PowerPoint presentation was cued up on the presentation computer. Beth's presentation, one of five presentations being given that day, was scheduled fourth on the list with a pitch time of 10:45 a.m., but since all the pitchers were encouraged to attend the other presentations, she arrived at 8:45 a.m. so that she'd be there for the first pitch at 9 a.m. In the lobby, she met the other entrepreneurs and business owners who were pitching that day. Two companies were pure start-ups like hers, meaning they were still in idea phase and had not yet launched a product or service. The first was run by a man with a radical design for ergonomic desk chairs. The second was a trio of twenty-somethings with a new app to facilitate carpools and ridesharing for working moms with active kids. The other three were established businesses. They included a restaurant owner who needed funding to open a second location, a sister and brother team that produced a regionally successful all-natural snack product that they wanted to take into national distribution, and the owner of a well-known, nationally-recognized web design firm who was ready to retire and wanted to sell his business to a couple of his employees who needed financial help to fund the ownership transition.

While Beth and her fellow entrepreneurs were waiting to be brought in, they all shared some tips they'd learned about the process from mentors and previous pitchers. The team from the snack company had gotten money from the fund before and said that the investment committee was very strict about the 12-minute pitch time. "They'll cut you off midsentence when the timer bell rings," the brother said. The restaurant owner said he'd heard that this panel was known for asking questions that are tough but fair. "Be prepared to defend your numbers," he warned. One of the twenty-something app designers added, "I have a friend who was successfully funded last year, and he said that if they kept you there the full 18 minutes with questions, you're in good shape. If you get done early, they're probably not interested."

"Great, more things to worry about," thought Beth as Jed ushered them into the auditorium. The committee included three men and two women, ranging in age from mid-30s to early 60s. The committee members were seated in the first row of the audience, and the seats behind them were filled almost to capacity. The pitch session was open to the public and member-investors in the fund were encouraged to attend. One of the original features of the fund was the creation of a proprietary app that allowed member-investors to contribute comments, questions, and (non-binding) votes of confidence to the committee. This helped the investment committee incorporate the "wisdom of the crowd" into their deliberations.

Jed indicated seats near the stage steps for each of the presenters and then headed onto the stage toward a podium that stood beside a large projection screen. He welcomed the committee members and the audience then briefly described the process. Each entrepreneur or business owner would be given 12 minutes to present their pitch, and they could use the projector and screen if they'd brought a PowerPoint deck or video. The pitch would then be followed by 18 minutes of Q&A with the investment committee, with Jed acting as moderator and timekeeper for the whole process.

Jed closed by saying, "As always, it's great to see so many member-investors here today, and this is your friendly reminder to help us stick to the tight schedule by submitting your feedback and questions via the DueD app on your phone or tablet. We highly encourage applause at the end of a presentation, but otherwise, remember you're silent partners in this process." Jed chuckled to himself as he waited for the customary response from some of the younger members of the crowd: "We love the DueD, dude!"

Before getting started with pitches, he called the investment committee up on stage and turned the mic over to MCF Investment Committee Chair, Erik Dakin. Erik gave a brief bio of his professional background, then stated why he was an investor and part of the investment committee. They went down the line of the rest of the committee members who did the same. It was a varied group, consisting of a retired marketing director, a real estate agent, a former banker turned stay-at-home-mom, a science teacher at

Moreland High School, and the owner of a string of carwashes in Moreland and surrounding towns. As they spoke, Beth started to realize they were ordinary people just like her. In fact, she recognized the stay-at-home-mom as a friend of her older sister who had graduated from Moreland State University four years ahead of Beth. The committee members' reasons for serving on the committee ran mostly along the lines of wanting to put their money to work for themselves as well as their community.

As she watched the first three presenters do their pitches and answer questions, she began to understand what the restaurant owner had meant by tough but fair questions. She was particularly impressed by the sister and brother team's calm response when the retired marketing director started asking very pointed questions about their plans for a national marketing campaign to sample their product at music venues. The sister responded, "We're partnering with a group of MBA (master of business administration) students at the university who are designing and implementing the program as part of their summer internship. We bought a used RV and will pay for their travel expenses plus a small stipend to each of them to sample our product at eight music festivals in six states over 10 weeks. The students are working to get sponsors whose logos will be painted all over the RV and whose funding will help cover the cost of our tent space at the events, and they're shipping the product to each venue. We believe this is smart business all around. Our sponsors get exposure on our RV and social media, the students get valuable hands-on experience that will earn them credit with their marketing professor, and we get our products in the hands of thousands of potential consumers."

As the sister and brother sat down, they high-fived each other, then the sister winked her support to Beth as she headed up to the stage. At first, Beth's voice was a little shaky as she started to introduce herself, but then she saw, sitting in the second row just behind the committee, her dog-park friend, Kieran, pantomiming a suggestion to breathe. She took a deep breath and launched into her well-rehearsed presentation. She ended with 10 seconds to spare on Jed's 12-minute timer, and he immediately opened the floor to the committee for questions. The retired marketing exec spoke up first, asking about Beth's target audience and outreach plan; the science teacher probed on the details of her technology and intellectual property; the former banker questioned her start-up cost estimates. Just as the real estate agent was about to ask a question, Jed signaled that time was up. "Wow that went fast," Beth thought as she took a deep breath and headed back to her seat. She acknowledged a couple thumbs up from the other presenters and smiled reassurance at the last presenter, and then she started mentally rehashing her answers as the ergonomic desk chair inventor launched into his pitch. She felt she'd done a pretty good job, but, now, only time would tell.

When the investment committee broke for lunch, all the presenters were surprised to find a buffet of sandwiches and salads set up for them in a small room off the auditorium. Jed told them this was something that an anonymous member-investor had insisted on and offered to pay for each session because he or she knew there was great benefit in entrepreneurs and businesspeople making connections and finding a peer group. Jed encouraged them to get to know each other, share contact information, and relax.

In about an hour, Beth and her fellow presenters were ushered into a classroom in a nearby building with tables and chairs set up in a circle with the MCF Investment Committee around one side and nametags in front of chairs for each of them. Jed again laid the groundwork for this part of the day. "This is the time for the investment committee to ask any final questions. Over lunch, they received feedback and further questions from member-investors in the audience, submitted through the DueD app. Also, this is your chance to ask questions of me or the committee."

Stephanie had prepared Beth for this last bit and said to have a couple questions ready. "This is not the time to be a wallflower," Stephanie advised. "It's another chance for them to get to know you and how you think. They're investing in YOU after all, not just your idea. Besides, you want to get to know them, too, and as much as you can about the fund's investors and its relationships with its other portfolio companies. If all goes well, the 1,237 investors in the fund will be stakeholders in your business. You don't have to know all of them personally or deal with them directly, but it's quite likely you WILL run into some of them in the grocery store. Ask the committee how ongoing interaction with the member-investors is managed. This is a relationship that could last many years, so make sure it's one you want. Be curious and cautious."

Beth learned a lot from hearing the answers to other people's questions and all the while, she was gathering her courage to ask what she thought might be a risky question. She was afraid it might show her ignorance or even her unwillingness to accept the fund as a partner, but it was something she really needed to understand if she was going to take its money. Finally, there was a lull, and she raised her hand, timidly at first but then confidently as she let it shoot all the way up to be seen. Erik gave her the floor and she began, "From what I learned on your website, it looks like you make investments either in the form of a revenue-share agreement or a convertible note that converts into a significant share of equity after three years. How do you decide which one, and do I get any say in what I would want?"

"Great question!" said Erik. "I'm going to let Jed handle that one."

Jed took over. "I'm always surprised when we have sessions where no one asks that question. The structure of an investment deal is a key factor in developing a good long-term relationship between you and the fund. And more important to you, of course, is the fact that the structure of a deal can have a huge impact on your company's ability to raise additional capital in the future. Typically, we reserve the revenue-share model for more established businesses that have proven cash flow. In a case like yours and a couple others around the table who are pure start-ups or earlier stage businesses, a convertible note with potential for an equity stake makes more sense—for both the company and the fund."

"Ok, I get that much, but what do you mean by a significant share of equity? I'll be honest, it kind of feels like I'm losing my company before I even begin!" Many of her fellow entrepreneurs nodded in agreement.

"It's important here to distinguish the difference between ownership and control," Jed began. "While we take a significant ownership stake, we leave the control and the day-to-day management to you and your team. This is why we spend so much time getting to know you. We invest in companies that we believe have a great idea AND a great team to make it happen. We're not here to tell you how to run your business. We're here to help and support you when we can because we see this investment as a long-term relationship.

"Also, an important feature of our equity agreement is that you can buy back ownership over time. It's designed so that you get the capital you need to get started without the burden of loan payments or even revenue-sharing requirements, so you can devote all your early cash flow to building the business. Then, once you're profitable, you can choose to liquidate the equity interest through a payout system similar to a revenue-sharing arrangement. Many founders choose to do this after they feel the business is in a stable position cash-wise. But others choose to just keep the equity position and make an ownership transfer to employees at some point in the future. At that time, the fund gets its payday. It really depends on your long-term goals for the company and the part you want to play within it. Besides, you don't have to decide today about the buyback provision. That's something we just keep on the back burner until the time is right to talk about it."

"Wow, this is all so refreshing," said the ergonomic desk chair entrepreneur. "I've been talking with friends of mine in San Francisco who're on the angel investor circuit trying to raise money for their company, and they said it feels very adversarial, like they're David to the rich guy's Goliath."

"That's why we say our fund is neighborly capital," replied a member of the investment committee. "We have a vested interest to see your company grow and be successful, not just so that we, the investors, benefit financially, but also so that Moreland benefits from the jobs you create and from the products or services you provide. There's also the extended economic impact when you source from or engage with other local businesses. Your business needs might even inspire the creation of new companies to support it. This is why we include a "Long-Term Local" clause in all of our investment deals that requires a company to repay the outstanding balance of our investment plus 15% interest immediately upon a decision to relocate beyond 50 miles of Moreland's city line. We want to encourage businesses to stay local to create a virtuous cycle of wealth throughout our community for years to come."

Another committee member chimed in, "And because this fund represents the community and its support for you, we also have an expectation that your business will be a good corporate citizen by making good choices with regard to environmental and social responsibilities and by encouraging civic engagement. We believe this is very important for the long-term health and welfare of our city and its citizens, which, in turn, is good for business. This might sound like a lot of expectations but think about the benefits: You're getting patient capital with fair terms from people who could become your biggest fans and brand ambassadors. When you succeed, the fund benefits, and so does Moreland. It's a win-win-win."

Beth smiled at these words that echoed Stephanie's description of the fund. After a few more technical questions from the entrepreneur group, Jed announced the end, at least for the entrepreneurs, of the pitch day. After a short break, the committee would reconvene for their final deliberations and recommendations. He sent the presenters away with congratulations on a good day and the promise that each of them could expect an email from him by noon the following Saturday.

The following week at work was torture as Beth tried to focus on her projects at Holland while trying to resist the urge to check her personal email every hour to see if Jed's response might come early. True to his word, at noon on Saturday, an email popped up on her phone with a subject line that read, "Next Steps: MCF and Door Tudor, Inc." This sounded promising. The email read:

> Dear Beth,
>   Thank you for being a part of Moreland Community Fund's Pitch Day. We'd like to move forward with an investment. The proposed details can be found in the attached term sheet. Please review with your attorney at your earliest convenience and set a time to meet me at the MCF office to discuss. Your attorney is welcome to join. In the meantime, feel free to send any questions my way.
>   Best,
>   Jed

Over the next two weeks, Beth and her attorney worked with Jed to sort out the details of the Fund's $40,000 investment in Door Tudor, Inc. Like most of the investments the Fund made, it would be structured as a convertible note into an equity investment, and both Jed and her attorney advised that she use the same terms for F&F investments as well as her own, which made up the remaining $20,000 for Door Tudor's start-up capital. At first, even after Jed's explanation of ownership versus control the week before, she was still a little wary of giving up a percentage of her company after the conversion. He could tell by her body language that this was bothering her and reiterated, "The Fund does NOT want to run your company. We want YOU to run your company and to hire great managers and teammates as you grow along the way. Our role is to provide the funding now to help you get going and to help you find growth capital along the way as you need it. If you do your job well, which is launching, growing and managing this company, we can make it easier for you to find the capital you need in the future. In essence, we're lifting some of the burden of constantly raising capital from your shoulders so you can focus on what you're going to do best: run your company."

This sealed the deal in Beth's eyes. Within a week, she was saying goodbye to her friends at Holland & Sons and hello to her new workspace (formerly the guest bedroom in her small house). After three months,

Door Tudor had its first customers—one of whom was an investor in the MCF, who'd learned about her innovative distribution model in the Fund's quarterly newsletter. By the end of the first 12 months in business, Beth had hired a new employee and moved the company operations into a dedicated office in Moreland's downtown coworking space.

Door Tudor had some growing pains in its second year as the company expanded to meet rapidly rising demand. True to his word, Jed helped Beth navigate her company's capital needs with a second round of funding, this time in the form of a revenue-share agreement, and helped her secure a line of credit from Moreland Mutual Savings Bank. By year four, Door Tudor was showing consistent monthly profits and started making regular revenue-share payments to the Fund.

Seven and a half years after Beth Tudor set out to launch her own company, she found herself once more sitting in an old familiar chair across the desk from John Holland. This time, they were joined by a pair of attorneys who spread two copies of thick legal documents in front of the former colleagues. As they each signed and then swapped documents for countersignatures, John looked up at Beth and said, "When I took over this company from my dad, I always imagined, someday, I'd turn it over to one of my kids. But as you know, Holland & Sons wasn't their cup of tea. I can't imagine anyone closer to a daughter than you, Beth, and it makes me so happy that you'll continue the Holland tradition as part of Door Tudor. Keep up the good work and call me if you need me but don't be surprised if my answering machine says I've gone fishing!"

Chapter 9

A Call to Action

The story of Beth Tudor and the MCF is something I wrote in the summer of 2018 as I pondered a pivot for Milk Money. It helped me see the possibilities of how a community could work together to make its own economy stronger and more resilient without waiting for handouts, or bailouts, or outside help in general. I haven't shared this story with anyone until now, but the underlying concepts of it started seeping into the exploratory work I was doing with the nonprofit I started in the spring of 2018. Launched initially to take over and augment the investor education work started by Milk Money, the Initiative for Local Capital (or Local Cap, for short) is an innovation lab with a mission to create democratic investment opportunities, educational tools and resources, and inclusive networks that support all members of a community to invest where their hearts and homes are.

Part of the project work I laid out for Local Cap in the fall of 2018 was the creation of a Vermont-wide community investment fund. Through a grant proposal that I wrote for the project, a serendipitous connection was made, and, by February 2019, I found myself working on a real-life version of the MCF: the Northeast Kingdom (NEK) Prosperity Fund designed to serve three remotely rural and economically challenged counties in northeastern Vermont. The NEK Prosperity Fund is one of just a handful of pioneers in the field of community investment funds that I'll talk about more in a bit, but, first, I want to share one last story. A true one. It's the story of how I set myself on this path in the first place, and it is my touchstone when the going gets rough on the entrepreneurial path I've chosen.

Way back in 2004, when I was still working at Seventh Generation, the company participated in the Green Festival in Washington D.C., a trade show of sorts that was open to the public so they could come learn about all the ways they could "green up" their homes and their lifestyle. My job was to staff the Seventh Generation booth and encourage passersby to take samples of our natural, non-toxic dish liquid and laundry detergent, so they could try them at home. A guy came up to the booth who didn't need any encouragement—he was already a big fan of Seventh Generation. So big, in fact, that he was ready to take his relationship with the company to a new level; he asked if he could invest in Seventh Generation.

"Wow, that's so cool!" I exclaimed. "But . . . I have no idea how, or even if, that would work. Let me go find our CEO, Jeffrey Hollender. He's the one who deals with this kind of stuff." I had to search a bit before

I found Jeffrey behind our booth in a conversation with Seventh Generation's Vice President of Sales. Jeffrey was not quite as excited as I was about the prospect, probably because he knew, after years of raising capital from professional angel investors and venture capital funds, that big checks don't materialize out of thin air at a Green Festival. He was also instantly cautious, rightfully so, because he knew the delicate legal consequences around raising money from individuals. Thus, the first thing he said I had to do was ask if the guy was an accredited investor, and he gave me the rough definition because I sure didn't know! The guy didn't know either, and after I told him it meant someone with $1 million in net worth (not including his home) and/or $200,000 of annual income, I watched in awkward silence as his body language communicated first his disappointment and then his embarrassment. We were both a bit crestfallen and we fumbled for a graceful way to end the conversation. I offered him as many samples as he could carry, and he quickly walked away.

I came away from that experience with a sense of injustice for having to deny someone the ability to use his money in a way that felt good and right to him, simply because he didn't have enough of it to satisfy the SEC's definition of a suitable investor. The restriction on unaccredited investors stems from the Securities Act of 1933 and was put in place to protect the average citizen from scam artists and other unscrupulous actors.

A worthwhile endeavor to be sure, but a perhaps unforeseen byproduct is the institutionalization over nearly 100 years of a system where only the wealthy are deemed "sophisticated" (i.e., intelligent, rational, able to make wise decisions) enough to do with their money as they please. As a finance professor at a prestigious MBA program once commented to me, "Even though I'm a widely recognized expert on financial systems and markets, I'm barred from making direct local investments because I haven't yet amassed enough wealth for the SEC to believe in my intelligence."

This finance professor, and the rest of us in the 95% of unaccredited American households, have to take what Wall Street offers us. This system is what I have been trying to change for 15 years, and I'm heartened to see changes finally being made to regulations that were put in place before most of us were born. But more needs to change.

In order to make the American Dream of economic opportunity available for anyone with vision, drive, and ingenuity, we must find ways for all of us to participate equally in the system. Unfortunately, our current system works all too well . . . for a privileged few (many of whom are reluctant to make changes that might lessen their privilege.) At the risk of sounding extreme, I'll go so far as to compare our current capital system to the feudal system of the middle ages wherein rich landowners got richer off the labor of those who worked the land as tenant farmers. Now, I know our capital markets are not as completely oppressive and overtly established as the feudal system, but for women, people of color, and others shut out from the benefits of deeply entrenched privilege, it can certainly feel like there's no way to break free of the cycle. In today's terms, these marginalized entrepreneurs have to rely on the "moneyed gentry" for the funding to get an entrepreneurial venture off the ground, and then they end up watching as the lion's share of the profits go back to those who controlled all the money in the first place.

So how do we break the cycle? This is not a call to redistribute wealth from the rich to the poor. In fact, I am specifically NOT advocating for the redirection of angel and venture capital funds into investments in women, people of color, rural business owners, and other disenfranchised entrepreneurs. To do so would simply perpetuate the patriarchal system of the rich getting richer off the labor of the poor as the extractive angel/venture capital model continues to expect 10 times (or higher) returns on investment.

What I'm talking about is a very different system altogether. One that starts with the fundamental question of why someone is investing in the first place. Is it simply to grow one's personal portfolio? Or could there be a driving desire to support greater economic prosperity for one's self AND our local economy? A key difference between my first question and the second is that in the first scenario, success is measured solely in terms of dollars, whereas in the second, financial return is just one measure of success comingled with others such as quality job creation, sustainable use of resources to create useful goods and services, wealth recirculation through relationships with other local businesses, and greater civic engagement. Are these latter benefits acceptable as ROI? Can they be just as compelling to an investor as watching one's portfolio grow?

Imagine a miser sitting alone among his evergrowing piles of gold, which he hoards down in a vault. His only intent with his investments is to create more wealth that he can then bring back and store away in his vault where it's doing nothing productive other than giving him the joy of counting it. If everyone, like this miser, is concerned only with growing their own piles of money—even if they use some of it for charitable purposes—it is mostly just dead money sitting there gathering dust in a vault. To bring this into real world terms of today, those piles of gold equate to securities. A large part of most portfolios is invested in pieces of paper known as stocks, bonds, and mutual funds. These pieces of paper—or securities as they're known collectively—represent a form of ownership or other financial claim on the companies that issue them. For most of us who hold these securities indirectly by investing in mutual funds, unless we're willing to dive deep into the microscopic print of our mutual fund prospectuses, we have no idea what companies we've invested in, and they could be doing who knows what with our money. The rise in socially responsible investing that began in the 1960s, and more recently, ESG investment practices that focus on environmental, social, and governance measures, has helped raise awareness of the connection between capital and social good. Still, with most ESG mutual funds and portfolio management techniques, you're mostly just screening out the really bad actors rather than actively supporting companies with deeply ingrained social missions.

And speaking of actively supporting companies with deeply ingrained social missions, when you invest in publicly traded securities like stocks, bonds, and mutual funds, unless it's an IPO, your money isn't even going directly to the underlying company to support its work. It's just going to someone else who bought the security before you and now wants to sell it.

So what are the alternatives? Crowdfunding is certainly a new alternative and an important step in the right direction. Crowdfunding gives each of us the ability to put our dollars where our values are by investing directly in companies that we believe will contribute to the common good as well as to our own good. But as we've seen, there are limitations to crowdfunding in its current form that I believe will keep it from being the magic pill to cure all of our money system's ills. I'm hopeful yet skeptical that crowdfunding platforms will find a way to make direct investment broadly available and financially feasible; and in the meantime, I and others are exploring ways to achieve the same end by moving the activity from the individual to the community level.

Margaret Mead probably didn't have community investing in mind when she said, "Never doubt that a small group of thoughtful, committed citizens can change the world; indeed, it's the only thing that ever has,"[30] but the concept certainly holds true in this case. In fact, the power of small groups of thoughtful, committed citizens is exactly what I'm talking about when I say that Main Street Americans can move mountains. The 1% may have a lock on the vast majority of wealth in this country, but there's still an awful lot that the rest of us can do if we combine our efforts. We have power in our numbers, too.

Americans have roughly $56 trillion invested in our retirement accounts, pensions, mutual funds, and insurance funds, most of which is invested in publicly traded corporations.[31] The reason for this is that, until very recently, publicly traded securities were the only things that unaccredited Americans could feasibly (and often, legally) invest in. Indeed, when you're talking about a qualified retirement plan like a 401(k), 403(b), or a standard IRA, it is impossible to invest in anything other than publicly traded securities, due to restrictive SEC regulations.

A movement is afoot to make it easier for people to set up what's called a Self-Directed IRA (SDIRA) or a Solo 401(k), either of which allow for direct local investment of one's retirement funds. This is a huge step in the right direction. The pioneering efforts of groups like The Next Egg are helping to move things forward more rapidly. As this book went to print, a small group of trailblazing self-employed folks calling themselves The Next Egg's First Hatch (including your truly), was finalizing the legal documentation to start their Solo 401(k)s, with plans to begin investing in early 2020. As The Next Egg's website states, it is bringing together creative legal and economic minds who are devoted to "empowering ourselves to self-direct retirement savings toward building vibrant communities." The Next Egg cofounder, acclaimed author, and globally recognized expert on community economics, Michael Shuman, will also provide additional insight and guidance on SDIRAs and Solo 401(k)s in his forthcoming book, *Put Your Money Where Your Life Is*. Stay tuned!

A recent study estimates that roughly 83% of U.S. savings is held in retirement accounts like standard IRAs or workplace-sponsored retirement savings plans like 403(b)s and 401(k)s.[32] So until the SEC and the Internal Revenue Service (IRS) decide to make some much needed regulatory changes—or until SDIRAs and Solo 401(k)s are easier to set up—we're stuck, right? Not necessarily. For one thing, at least some of the remaining 17% of our savings is in regular savings accounts, money market accounts, or certificates of deposit. So an easy first step is to move some of that money to a locally owned bank or credit union. This is perhaps the easiest step you can take, yet it packs a powerful punch.

To understand how, let's start with the notion of banks that are "too big to fail."[33] I'm not going to delve into whether the government's actions in the wake of the global financial crisis of 2008 were right or wrong at the time. I want to look at the long-term effect of giving big banks a Get Out of Jail Free card (literally and figuratively). By demonstrating that some institutions are deemed so essential to the functioning of our economy that they can't be allowed to collapse, regardless of the cost to the U.S. taxpayer, we have basically given them a blank check to continue their bad behavior. This is called *moral hazard*, a term that came into broad usage by English insurance companies in the late 1800s, and it occurs when someone increases their exposure to risk because they know they are insured. For example, a street performer might say, "I'll use my grandmother's valuable antique vase in my juggling act because if it breaks, I can collect the insurance money."

Moral hazard is taken to the extreme when a person takes even more risk because someone else bears the cost of that risk. In the case of our street juggler, maybe she adds in her grandmother's fine china because she knows her grandparents already paid for the insurance years ago, but she will be the only person to collect on the claim now. The global financial crisis of 2007–2008 was caused in large part by banks taking huge risks on mortgage loans that never should have been made, and now that these "too big to fail" banks have been bailed out with taxpayer money (and most of them are doing just fine by the way, reporting booming profits in 2018), what is to keep them from taking more, and more daring, risks in the future?[34] Now that we have a precedent of bailing them out, does the allure of otherwise risky behavior become overwhelmingly attractive?

This is, of course, a huge and complex issue, and the responsibility for solving it might seem to reside with the Federal Reserve Board, or other federal regulatory agencies, or Congress, or someone else with the will and colossal power required to rein in the bad behavior of big banks. There's nothing you or I can do other than barraging our congressional representatives with email or setting up our tent to Occupy Wall Street, right? While these actions certainly have merit, I'm going to propose something even easier and perhaps more permanently effective in the long run.

These big banks are only big if we give them our money to play with in the first place. What if we took our marbles and went home? Literally. There are other banking alternatives out there in the form of locally owned mutual savings banks and credit unions.

Local banks and credit unions are far more likely to make loans to small local businesses than are big national banks. This not only keeps money circulating locally but also keeps key decision-making power in your community. The sad truth is that since 2008, when we first started talking about banks that were too big to fail, one in four local banks has shut its doors. In fact, since 1995 when small- and medium-sized banks and credit unions made up nearly half (48%) of the market, their market share plummeted to 23% by 2014. They're now dwarfed by four mega-banks, Citigroup, JP Morgan Chase, Wells Fargo, and Bank of America. These four banks, together, control 38% of the total banking market.[35]

Still, there are many options for local banking, and the seemingly small step of moving money out of a mega-bank and into a local one is not only the easiest way to take more control of your money, it's also often a very wise financial move personally. Small banks are far more likely to offer free checking and have lower fees than the large banks (large banks are defined as having more than $10 billion in assets), and small banks often offer higher interest rates on savings accounts and certificates of deposit.[36] A Think Local nonprofit organization in the seacoast region of New Hampshire and Maine created an online tool to help you find one close to you. On the homepage of BankLocal.info you simply type in your zip code, and up pops a list of banks in your region that are rated on their impact, which is evaluated by the amount of small business lending they do, their ownership structure, and even whether they engage in speculative lending.

What if millions of us took the baby step of opening a savings account or buying a certificate of deposit at one of these local banks or credit unions? It's an easy step; you don't have to move all your banking to a local bank (unless you want to, which I highly encourage). Just start with a savings account, which can often be opened with as little as $25. Such a move not only takes money out of the gambling hands of big banks, but provides a much more positive benefit because local banks and credit unions put that money to work in local economies by lending to small businesses that are the backbone of the U.S. economy.

I believe this statement that is currently posted on BankLocal.info, sums it up perfectly: "The primary activity of almost all small banks and credit unions is to turn deposits into loans and other productive investments. Meanwhile, big banks devote a sizeable share of their resources to speculative trading and other Wall Street bets that may generate big profits for the bank, but provide little economic or social value for the rest of us and can put the entire financial system at risk if they go bad."

Ok, so now that I've convinced you to save local by changing where you bank, let's talk about going deeper with other forms of community capital. The concept of community capital in the U.S. is not a new one. In the 1960s, President Johnson's War on Poverty led to the creation of community loan funds in the 1970s–80s. These community loan funds were funded largely by wealthy individuals and religious organizations to provide loans and other financial support to low-income communities. The number and size of community loan funds grew slowly over the next 10–20 years until Clinton-era legislation in the mid 1990s created the Community Development Financial Institution Fund within the U.S. Treasury Department, giving the CDFI industry a significant boost.

Today, the CDFI Fund provides federal funding to registered community development financial institutions, 51% of which are community loan funds. Community loan funds play an important role in the financing landscape for small businesses, especially in low-income communities. Unfortunately, many do not accept investments from unaccredited investors, which, again, excludes most Americans from participating in these community investment opportunities.

There are some exceptions: Vermont Community Loan Fund, New Hampshire Community Loan Fund, Mountain BizWorks in North Carolina, the Boston Impact Initiative, and PVGrows Fund in Massachusetts. All of these accept investments from citizens from all walks of life and allow them to participate in the great work they're doing with their lending efforts to fund economic growth within their respective regions. There is also a growing trend toward the establishment of community investment funds that would not only allow unaccredited investors but also provide a broader array of investment opportunities (i.e., equity or near-equity) for entrepreneurs and start-ups that need more than just another loan fund. This is an exciting development that warrants a whole chapter to itself.

Chapter 10

Manifesto

A trend toward the creation of community investment funds that allow unaccredited investors to aggregate funds and then invest together is just starting to emerge. I believe funds like these will be an effective response to both the promised opportunities and the perceived limitations of crowdfunding and are a viable pivot toward true community capital. Crowdfunding opened the door for anyone, regardless of wealth status, to make direct investments into start-ups and local businesses. However, the fly in the ointment with crowdfunding is that direct local investment is a big step for many people; it's possibly too big a step to support large-scale adoption.

For someone like my friend Marco Vangelisti, it was perhaps not so challenging to move his entire portfolio into local investments because he'd had years of training and experience in evaluating investment opportunities. As a former professional portfolio manager, he already spoke the language and had a certain comfort level with financial data. All of these factors gave him a big leg up when you consider the jargon-full language of the financial world—not to mention the dizzying array of spreadsheets one is supposed to review. To an intelligent, thoughtful person whose expertise is focused on something other than analyzing financial projections all day long, the prospect of making your own investment decisions can be daunting.

But wait a minute, you say. If we are aiming to rebalance our priorities away from investing solely in order to create more wealth for ourselves, does it still require becoming a financial whiz kid? Perhaps not a whiz kid, but you can't ignore the numbers altogether; I'll walk you through some common sense ways to review financial projections below. But before we do that, let's consider another, perhaps better, way to evaluate potential investments. It may sound a little hokey, but what if we dare to invest with our hearts as well as our heads?

What does this mean? It means evaluating an investment opportunity on criteria other than just financial return. It means giving weight to the value of investing in business propositions that make us happy. For instance, investing in a smart, energetic woman named Kai Nortey who not only makes insanely delicious non-dairy ice cream from cold-pressed coconut cream, but does so with an intent to build an ethnically inclusive food justice and health economy in the Oakland Bay area of California. Her patent-pending equipment and proprietary chemical-free processing methods (that have "big ice cream" shaking in their shoes by the way), are the key to delivering the freshest ingredients for her "nice cream." A key part of this Black-owned, woman-led business is its mission to play a pivotal role in building regenerative economies that focus on food justice and the triple bottom line of restorative economics, racial and gender equity, and environmental sustainability.[37]

Kai is the founder of Kubé, based in Oakland, California, and along with all the standard sections of her business plan on market assessment, production model, sales and distribution strategy, and financial projections she includes the deeply integrated ways her business model will contribute to a new economy. Her guiding principles include things like using fresh, whole, plant-based ingredients that are processed without chemicals; hiring formerly incarcerated women who are survivors of domestic violence or human trafficking; and donating Kubé's coconut byproducts to make compost for urban community farms in East Oakland.[38]

Kai and Kubé just might be a great investment opportunity precisely because her business proposition makes you happy. An enthusiastic, engaging, and articulate leader with a product that is already attracting a loyal audience are two big boxes to check off on your due diligence list, after all. A group of friends, family, and fanatic followers seem to agree, as her successful $105,000 campaign on Crowdfund Mainstreet demonstrates.

Investing with our hearts *and* our heads also means including our conscience in our decision-making process. It means not sacrificing our integrity just because an investment might make us a lot of money. Unfortunately, portfolio managers of many nonprofit endowments and community foundations might find themselves inadvertently guilty of this, just as Marco Vangelisti once was as he directed investments for his client, the so-called protector of orangutans, into a company that clear-cut the habitat of those very same orangutans. It is not uncommon to hear these portfolio managers justify their investment strategies by stating that the more money they make, the more their clients can spend on their organization's philanthropic mission.

Individual investors can fall into the same trap with their personal portfolios; they rationalize that the more they make in the stock market, the more they can donate to philanthropy, and they never think about the impact of their investment strategy. Impact investing has been around for over ten years and generally refers to investments made with a specific intent to generate measurable and beneficial social or environmental results as well as positive financial returns. But a friend of mine, who is a thoughtful and intentional investor, told me recently she believes the term *impact investing* is a misnomer, pointing out that, "Every investment has an impact; what matters is knowing—and caring—whether the impact is positive or negative."

This is why I propose turning the due diligence process on its head to make our decisions based on whether an opportunity is going to satisfy needs like creating safe, good-paying, fulfilling jobs or, on an even more basic level, whether a company is producing goods or services that contribute to the overall well-being of people, a community, or the planet. Imagine the long-term benefits to society if more people invested with their conscience and supported businesses that create broad social benefits as well as positive financial returns. A corresponding outcome could be the defunding of businesses that do harm. Just like in the last chapter where we talked about how we can collectively change the banking system by taking our money out of big banks, we can do the same with our investments. By voting with our wallets we can have a significant impact on our economy, possibly even eradicating parts of it that contribute nothing positive or are, in some way, detrimental.

In colonial America, a business was given a corporate charter only if it could prove to a colony's legislature that it was being organized specifically for the common good. Corporate charters were intended to create and support entities that would contribute to a community's best interests, typically for civic projects like building roads and canals. As colonial legislatures became state legislatures, they retained the power to govern the amount of time for which a corporate charter was granted, and, importantly, could choose whether to renew an expiring charter or not. However, in the 100 years that followed the Revolutionary War and with the growth of our federal system of government, the laws regulating corporations were eventually relaxed. By the late 1800s, corporations no longer had to demonstrate their contribution to the common good to exist, and their years of operation were no longer limited.[39] Today, the act of forming a corporation is mostly a function of filing paperwork and paying some fees.

Imagine if the colonial model were reinstated. Would companies that produce violent video games exist? Would McDonald's still be in business considering our current state of epidemic childhood obesity? Would the pharmaceutical industry be worth billions of dollars?

For the colonial system to work today, there would have to be some kind of review board to oversee corporate operations and to decide who keeps their charter and who gets a smack down. I suppose this would be a government entity, ideally at the state or even local level. I kind of like the idea of this model and think it should be something we work toward for the future of our democratic society. However, I realize it would require lots of regulatory reform that deeply entrenched corporate lobbyists will fight tooth and nail against, so I won't hold my breath.

But I believe we can take steps toward making an informal review system happen right here, right now through the creation of organized groups of thoughtful citizen investors. They wouldn't have the power to revoke corporate charters, but they'd have the power to give or deny funding to businesses based on how a company's performance adhered to the investing group's values statement. A collective group of citizen investors would have the potent power of voting with their wallets. This could be game-changing as groups of citizens pool their money to make investments that are beneficial for their communities as well as their personal finances. Just the mere fact of moving their money out of traditional Wall Street investments into new Main Street funds would have a big impact. I've long said we can have greater impact not by occupying Wall Street but by defunding it—by taking our marbles and finding a new game. Without our money, investment bankers and big corporations have nothing left to play with. Let's take our money and put it to work according to our own rules.

But this is hard, you say. The financial world is complex and run by firmly established players with deep pockets and powerful lobbyists that will make it as hard as possible for us to leave their big games of marbles.

Let's tackle the second part of that statement first: Yes, there are firmly established players who will fight tirelessly to hold on to their power. But I'm betting that they don't see us, the individual Main Street Americans, as a threat to their power. They're too focused on the big clients and their big portfolios. How long would it take them to notice a whole bunch of small players leaving the game? Perhaps not until enough of those small players have added up to a meaningful amount, and by then, it could be too late for them to do anything about it.

So now, let's look at the first part of the statement: The financial world is complex. Some may say it is the inherent complexity of finance that has attracted so many of the best and brightest from America's MBA programs to Wall Street for the past 30–40 years. Only the super smart financial wunderkinds can understand this stuff, right? Actually, after reading plenty of works by Michael Lewis, I've concluded that the beeline from biz school to Wall Street works more like this: There's a lot of money to be made on Wall Street, which is what lured smart graduates there in the first place, and then to justify and perpetuate their existence, they created increasingly complex and arcane "products" that only they could understand. They are trying to be the Great and Powerful Oz, but we can pull back the curtain and discover it's just a frantic little man with a lot of smoke and mirrors. Just like Dorothy, there's a far simpler way to find our way home.

It's not quite as simple as clicking our ruby-slippered heels, but the words are the absolute right place to start: There's no place like home. What is it that makes Dorothy want to leave the glitzy, fantastical Emerald City? And what is the only way to make it happen? It is her vision of family, friends, a comfortable home, and a simple and sustainable existence. That is Dorothy's magic.

These are powerful attributes—family, friends, a comfortable home, a simple and sustainable existence—and ones that I believe are the keys to resilient local economies where wealth flows and circulates among all citizens. So how do we incorporate these attributes into our investment decision-making? We transform them into questions to ask prospective investees to help us get to the heart and soul of a business.

Following are six simple questions to ask a business owner in order to evaluate their prospective investment opportunity:

1. Who are you?
2. What do you do?
3. Why do you do it?
4. Who will want it?
5. How do you deliver it?
6. How do you make money?

First, it's very important to note the order of these questions. The money question is last for a reason. If you don't get a satisfactory answer to all the questions above it (especially #3: why do you do it?), the final question will not matter, and you can save yourself hours of needless financial analysis.

So, let's start with *questions 1–5*. You don't have to be an expert in a company's industry to evaluate the answers to these questions. In fact, this is the beauty of many lifestyle companies: Common sense, logic, and even gut instinct can get you to a place where you feel confident about whether a business proposition makes sense or not. If you find yourself asking, "Why would someone ever want (insert product/service here)?," it's a red flag. If you have a negative reaction to the entrepreneur or management team (i.e., you don't believe, trust, or even like them), that's another red flag. If their reason for doing what they do does not inspire you or in any way does not ring true, that's a big red flag. By evaluating an opportunity on these metrics first, you'll hone in on those that have the highest probability of delivering a market-worthy product, aligning with values that are important to you, and that you want to support with your investment. Then and only then do you need to move on to the part that most people dread: looking at the numbers.

I just want to interject here that this method I'm proposing is very different from how angel and venture capital investors evaluate investment opportunities. Without fail, they go straight to the financials, presumably to see if the numbers are compelling enough to warrant further investigation. I'm turning that on its head to suggest that having a good understanding of the nature of the company and the entrepreneur or management team's motivations are the appropriate first screen. Plus, my technique requires your financial evaluation efforts only after companies make it past this point in your due diligence process, which can save a lot of time and angst if financial analysis is not your jam.

So once a company has successfully made it through *questions 1–5*, it is indeed time to move on to the financial evaluation. You'll notice that *question 6* is not how much money will the company make but how do you make money. These are very different concepts. We're looking to see if the management team has a good handle on the costs to produce, distribute, and sell their goods or services and a reasonable estimation of the price that customers are willing to pay. The bottom line, then, comes from subtracting the former from the latter to see if there's anything left at the end of the day (or month/quarter/year). Thus, the simple notion of making money encompasses both the producing and the selling of a product or service and implies that there will be profit. (There has to be profit if the business is going to be sustainable in the long run.)

Ok, I hear you saying, "This makes sense theoretically, but who am I to know if a company is setting a good price or properly estimating all the costs? How do I know if their projected annual growth rate is realistic or not? When should I reasonably expect the company to break even and start generating profit?"

These are all good, important, and appropriate questions. The financial aspect of due diligence is, indeed, complicated, and, depending on the business or industry, could take some time and research to get you to a place with comfortable answers. Some investors may have the tenacity and interest to track down answers to their questions, but many others may decide it's just too much darn work. This is precisely why I have surmised that crowdfunding in its current incarnation will not live up to expectations. Yet, I also caution us not to give up on crowdfunding too quickly and want to circle back to the recommendation to band together into citizen investing groups, clubs, or even an official fund. Doing so not only pools money together to be able to make more and larger investments, it also reduces risk through diversification, and it creates the opportunity to share the work of identifying and evaluating each potential investment across a group of like-minded individuals, some of whom ideally have financial acumen and enthusiasm for analysis. Plus, working as a group can be a lot more fun.

For accredited investors, direct local investment can easily be accomplished by joining an angel group. But what if you're not an accredited investor? First of all, you're not alone, not by a long shot. In *Community Investment Funds: A How-To Guide for Building Local Wealth, Equity, and Justice,* Michael Shuman used IRS and U.S. Census data along with financial data from DQYDJ.com to estimate the number of accredited investors at around 5.5% of the population.[40] That works out to an awful lot of us unaccredited Main Street investors out there. There is strength in our numbers if we can find a way to work together, and that strength derives in no small part from the *wisdom of crowds*.

The concept of crowdfunding is built on the notion of the wisdom of crowds, an idea popularized in modern times by a book of the same name by James Surowiecki in 2004, but whose origin stretches back to Aristotle's theory of collective judgment. In a nutshell, the wisdom of crowds is the idea that large crowds of people are collectively smarter than individual experts. An often cited example of the wisdom of the crowd is the story of Francis Galton and the ox. In 1906, Mr. Galton, a renowned statistician, was intrigued by a competition to guess the weight of an ox at a country fair. Eight hundred people bought tickets to enter a guess; whoever guessed closest to the actual weight won a prize. After the fair, Galton borrowed the tickets to run statistical tests on the entries. He discovered that while the individual guesses varied widely, the average of those guesses (1,197 lbs.) was remarkably close to the actual weight (1,198 lbs.). A modern-day example of this is the TV show *Who Wants to Be a Millionaire* in which contestants can ask the audience for input to answer a question. When the contestant decides to go along with the audience's most popular response, the answer is correct 95% of the time.[41]

With crowdfunding, the wisdom of the crowd can be a potent evaluation of the market viability of an entrepreneur's product or service. The collective gut sense of a large group of investors on whether a particular product idea is compelling enough to drive sales could be far more accurate than a Wall Street industry analyst's precisely because these investors are also consumers who make decisions every day on the value of products they find on store shelves (or more likely, these days, on Amazon).

Of course, there is no guarantee that a crowd-approved product or service will translate into a business being successful. The other ingredients for success include a thorough business plan, reasonable financial projections, a talented and committed management team, and a solid sales and marketing strategy at the very least. This is where the practical reality of crowdfunding limits the ability of the wisdom of crowds to work effectively. Each individual investor has to do his or her own due diligence, evaluating an investment opportunity on the viability of its product, or service, as well as all those other criteria, too. This process takes time and also assumes they have access to all the information they need to do an evaluation. As we started to see in Chapter 7, this is where crowdfunding starts to lose its luster. It's a lot of work for an individual investor to seek out and evaluate opportunities, especially when we're talking about smallish investments of $250–$2,500. It's even more work to keep track of how each investment is performing.

Whether equity crowdfunding will pan out as people expect remains to be seen, but I'm still very bullish on the wisdom of the crowd and the democratic access to capital it can provide. I began this book with the bigger and broader question of how to fix the American Dream, and while equity crowdfunding platforms may not be the silver bullet answer, they have demonstrated strong proof that community investing could help fill the gap left by traditional capital sources. Investibule, an online hub for discovering investment opportunities across 30+ crowdfunding sites, recently published a study titled *Community Capital Trends 2019*. In this study, Investibule founders Amy Cortese and Arno Hesse provide some promising statistics. After reviewing 2,000 state- and federally-registered crowdfunding offerings from mid-2016 to mid-2019, they found that 66% of the 2,000 crowdfunding offerings met or surpassed their funding targets. Even more promising, women-led businesses achieved full funding 77% of the time, and offerings by people of color succeeded 75% of the time. Cortese and Hesse's conclusion: Community investing supports diversity and inclusion.

Crowdfunding has proven that Main Street Americans are willing to invest in start-ups. But is that because they are looking for the get rich quick outcome or because they see it as a long-term investing strategy? I think the answer is mixed. Whether they'd admit it or not, I believe a lot of people are looking to get in on the ground floor of the next Facebook and are hoping for a big "win the lottery" type of payday. But I also see signs that something bigger (and better) is possible, and this is where I see the early success of state-based sites like Milk Money and Hatch Oregon as much more promising. I find it promising mostly because the businesses that posted campaigns on these sites were not trying to be unicorns. Most of them are good solid business propositions looking to deepen their roots within a community while building a long-term business and seeking the community's support to do so. In other words, what they were seeking was community capital, and the state-based crowdfunding platforms on which they posted their campaigns seemed—at the time—like a good way to get it.

As we saw at the end of the last chapter, CDFIs and community loan funds are also sources of community capital and are doing great work, but they too have their limitations. By and large, most community loan funds do not accept investment from unaccredited investors. Also, by virtue of the fact that they are loan funds, they typically tend to lend to established businesses with a proven track record and a greater likelihood to be able to repay a loan. Thus, start-ups and early stage businesses are often out of luck when it comes to community loan funds. I'm not saying there's anything wrong with their model; CDFIs and community loan funds fill an important niche in small business financing, but more is needed. So if CDFIs have their limitations and if equity crowdfunding is too much work for individual investors, what are entrepreneurs and unaccredited investors to do?

While accredited investors can band together into an angel group to share information and pool money to invest together, it is still extremely difficult for Main Street investors to do so because the JOBS Act only changed rules under the Securities and Exchange Acts of 1933–1934. These were much needed changes, of course, but they didn't touch the regulatory system that governs organized group investing. The regulation of organizations that make investments (including investment clubs, community loan funds, and mutual funds, among others) falls to another (nearly as old) piece of legislation called the Investment Company Act of 1940. The 1940 Act has yet to receive an update like its older cousins, so its rules remain in place, making it extremely cumbersome, often impossible, for unaccredited investors to participate in community-scale group investing. The restrictions imposed by the 1940 Act, thus, perpetuate the privilege of the wealthy who can more easily form an investment group and often hire or elect from within a team of qualified people to oversee due diligence responsibilities. For the time being, Main Street investors continue to face a significant barrier to entry into direct local investing since all of the burden of finding deals, doing due diligence, and tracking investments falls on the individual's shoulders.

The model I created with the Moreland Community Fund in the story of Beth Tudor is my vision for the next evolutionary step for community capital. A community-scale mutual fund that aggregates investments from anyone, regardless of wealth status, and that allows some degree of professional management in addition to investor involvement in decision-making is not out of the realm of possibility. We're starting to see baby steps in this direction with the creation of community investment funds that are finding ways to operate within the current limitations of the Investment Company Act of 1940. Oakland's East Bay Permanent Real Estate Cooperative and the Ujima Fund in Boston are two that are already in operation. Both are designed to include unaccredited investors alongside accredited investors and institutions and may have the ability to provide investments into businesses in forms other than loans. A few other pioneering funds are getting started around the country and testing the boundaries of the current regulations, but there is still a long way to go.

In early 2020, a handbook, *Community Investment Funds: A How-To Guide for Building Local Wealth, Equity, and Justice*, will be published with the goal to inspire more communities to aggregate capital for community wealth-building. The handbook was made possible through a joint effort of the Solidago Foundation and the National Coalition for Community Capital (NC3). I coauthored the handbook along with Michael

Shuman, Amy Cortese, and Brian Beckon. The four of us also helped launch NC3 in September 2017 with a mission to help build vibrant, equitable, and resilient local economies through the strategies of community capital. (Brian and I continue to serve on the board of NC3.) The handbook provides case studies of 10 community investment funds and describes the various legal structures that a community investment fund can utilize under the existing federal regulation. The handbook also provides a step-by-step guide to creating a community investment fund and details the necessary resources to launch and run a fund.

As more community investment funds come into being and demonstrate their effectiveness, as more of us move even small sums of money out of big banks and into credit unions and locally owned banks, as more of us invest in just one local business through an equity crowdfunding site or by direct investment, we will start a groundswell of money flowing into communities that creates a regenerative cycle of wealth that delivers a social ROI to the community as well as a financial ROI to ourselves. And we will have the proof to take to Washington, D.C. to make much needed changes to the 80-year-old Investment Company Act of 1940; changes that allow greater freedom and control for unaccredited investors over their money.

Statistics on the increasing concentration of wealth in the U.S. are often cited in current media with a sense of inevitability as if the widening wealth gap is an unsolvable conundrum unless drastic and voluntary (and highly unlikely) changes are made by those with most of the wealth. In 2010, Ralph Nader wrote a book of historical fiction, *Only the Super-Rich Can Save Us*, that described his vision for what this could look like. I don't disagree that change by the super-rich is necessary; perpetuating the rich-getting-richer is bad for all of us, and something's gotta give. And I fully support the work of groups like the Patriotic Millionaires, proud and self-proclaimed "traitors to their class" who are working to build a more stable, prosperous, and inclusive nation,[42] and the Resource Generation, a multiracial membership community of young people with wealth and/or class privilege who are committed to the equitable distribution of wealth, land, and power.[43]

But I'm also not willing to wait for the super-rich to save us. This book is my manifesto. It describes the steps I'm taking personally and professionally to make positive change in the world right now. I offer it to you as a catalyst to take steps in your own life. This book also documents my commitment to continue innovating, inspiring, and illuminating new models designed to unite the 1% and the 99% for 100% community capital; a change that will finally render the outdated, extractive, biased models obsolete.

As more of us awaken to our collective power to make small but coordinated actions, we will realize how we, the people, can bring about true economic justice and create a more sustainable future. This is an invitation to take the first step, because together we can move mountains.

Acknowledgments

This book would not have happened without the gentle yet persistent nudges over many years from Laurie Farrington. Laurie knew, long before I did, that I was capable of writing a book. She also introduced me to Paula Diaco, a fairy godmother to author-preneurs whose gifts stretch far beyond creating story arcs and developing a consistent writing practice. Her ever-growing portfolio of resources on how to build a writing platform are already proving indispensable as I launch this book and plan for the next.

A huge debt of gratitude goes to my friend, Tim Patterson, who, over a cup of tea in Craftsbury, Vermont, expressed enthusiasm for my topic and generously offered his editing skills. His facility with phrasing and affinity with my audience helped smooth the rough edges of my manuscript.

My quest for copyediting and graphic design support introduced me to one new friend and reconnected me with an old one. I met Vanessa Daunais through Onion River Press, and her copyediting skills not only improved my manuscript but taught me a lot about writing, editing, and reading. Michelle Hobbs and I met ages ago when we were each running our first businesses. Serendipity brought us together again right when I needed a graphic designer and she was seeking a re-entry into the world of book cover design. Michelle's insight and talent has brought the book's concept to life in ways I never imagined. Many thanks to both of you.

I first "met" Michael Shuman and Amy Cortese as an avid reader of their respective books. I've since had the pleasure of becoming their fellow co-founder of the National Coalition for Community Capital, a co-author on what I hope is the first of many projects on community investment funds, and their friend. Their mentorship as I took my first steps toward becoming an author has been invaluable.

Appreciation to Rachel Fisher at Onion River Press for her advice and guidance that helped me feel not quite so alone in the self-publishing process. Next time, remind me to hire an interior layout designer!

To Louisa Schibli, my fellow trailblazer in equity crowdfunding in the Wild West days before Title III, thank you for seeing the possibilities in my crazy CSE experiments, for taking the entrepreneurial leap with me, and for your continued work to support entrepreneurs, especially women, in Vermont. The community capital movement would not be where it is today without your commitment and innovation.

To Liz Scott, I tried to track you down as I wrote

about Liz Lovely, but to no avail. I did my best to represent your story in a forthright and fact-based manner, drawing upon research in publicly available resources, plus my own memories of our brief interaction. I am truly sorry that Milk Money couldn't help save your company and wish you the best in your "life after Liz Lovely."

This wouldn't be a book about crowdfunding without the support of all those who pre-bought a copy through my iFundWomen campaign in the fall of 2019, plus a handful of early supporters via Inlu.com way back in 2012. Thank you all for believing I could actually pull this off. Special thanks to:

- Jill Davies – who invests with her heart as well as her money to support women entrepreneurs.
- Jodi Harrington – whose entrepreneurial spirit never ceases to amaze and delight me.
- Courtney Lightfoot – without whom I could not have survived the start-up days of TrueBody. Thank you for helping me learn how to be a good entrepreneur, a better manager, and the best human being I can be.
- Amy Luster – so much more than business school study partner, cycling and skiing companion, and covert matchmaker. I value your insights on business issues and your wisdom on mothering, and, of course, your friendship.

- Sascha Mayer – the mastermind behind Mamava and its culture-changing innovations. Thank you for going far enough down the road with crowdfunding to set the stage for Milk Money.
- Kai Nortey – a rising star and shining example of social entrepreneurism and business savvy. You'll go far, my friend, and I'll be cheering you all the way.
- Sue Padien – one of my oldest and dearest friends whose fun-loving spirit is exceeded only by her kind and generous heart. You've seen me at my best and my worst, and remain steadfast.
- Ethan Pomerance – whose vision for community capital and ability to connect important dots will catalyze results I can't wait to see.
- Abbott Stark – the creative and astute entrepreneur of a beautiful brand, and a fine human being to boot. I watch Ogee's continued success with pride and pleasure.

Finally, and most important, thank you to my family, Chip, Anna, and Katie Betz, who weathered some tough storms during the TrueBody years and stuck by me all the same. Your patience and support as I first tested my wings as an entrepreneur and now as a writer mean more to me than you may ever know. Thank you for allowing me to discover my true calling. And to the furry member of our family: Thank you, Willow, for pulling me away from my computer and into the woods for fresh air and perspective when I needed it most.

ENDNOTES

Introduction
1. Akhilesh Ganti, "Angel Investor," Investopedia, August 21, 2019, https://www.investopedia.com/terms/a/angelinvestor.asp.

Chapter 2
2. "History," Fred Meyer, accessed January, 27, 2020, https://www.fredmeyer.com/topic/history-2.

Chapter 4
3. Milton Friedman, *Capitalism and Freedom*, (Chicago: University of Chicago Press), 133.
4. "Dr. David Brower Biography," Architects for Peace Foundation, accessed January 20, 2020, http://www.architectsofpeace.org/architects-of-peace/david-brower.

5. Special Report: "A heavyweight champ, at five foot two: The legacy of Milton Friedman, a giant among economists," *The Economist*, November 23, 2006, https://www.economist.com/special-report/2006/11/23/a-heavyweight-champ-at-five-foot-two.
6. Architects for Peace Foundation, "Dr. David Brower Biography."
7. "Sustainable Investing Trends in 2019 and 2018 ESG Performance," Sustainable Research and Analysis LLC, accessed January 27, 2020, https://www.sustainableinvest.com/2019-esg-investing-trends/.
8. "History," Social Venture Circle, accessed January, 20, 2020, https://www.svcimpact.org/about/history/.
9. "Frequently Asked Questions about Small Business," Small Business Administration, September 2012, pg. 1, https://www.sba.gov/sites/default/files/FAQ_Sept_2012.pdf.
10. *Wall Street*, directed by Oliver Stone (1987; Los Angeles, CA; Twentieth Century Fox)
11. Ron Lieber, "One Money Question to Rule Them All: How Much Is Enough?" *New York Times*, November 24, 2016, https://www.nytimes.com/2016/11/24/

your-money/one-money-question-to-rule-them-all-how-much-is-enough.html.
12. Bob Dylan, "Like a Rolling Stone," track #1 on Highway 61 Revisited, Columbia Records, 1965, studio album.

Chapter 5

13. Dan D'Ambrosio, "Vermont cookie maker Liz Lovely vanished without a trace. What happened?" *Burlington Free Press*, August 10, 2018, https://www.burlingtonfreepress.com/story/money/2018/08/10/shark-tank-fail-vermont-butcher-block-liz-lovely-cookies-entrepreneur-mark-cuban-reality-abc-tv/949931002/.
14. D'Ambrosio, "Liz Lovely."
15. D'Ambrosio, "Liz Lovely."
16. D'Ambrosio, "Liz Lovely."
17. Valentina Zarya, "Female Founders Got 2% of Venture Capital Dollars in 2017," *Fortune*, January 31, 2018, https://fortune.com/2018/01/31/female-founders-venture-capital-2017/.
18. Gené Teare, Ned Desmond, "Announcing the 2017 update to the Crunchbase Women in Venture report," TechCrunch, October 4, 2017, https://techcrunch.com/2017/10/04/an

nouncing-the-2017-update-to-the-crunchbase-women-in-venture-report/.
19. Susan Price, "As Entrepreneurship Thrives, Women are Starting More Innovative Businesses than Men," *Forbes*, November 15, 2017, https://www.forbes.com/sites/susanprice/2017/11/15/as-entrepreneurship-thrives-women-are-starting-more-innovative-businesses-than-men/#2d678e313da5.
20. Jeff Cornwall, "Female entrepreneurs and the 'lifestyle business'," *The Christian Science Monitor*, February 28, 2011, https://www.csmonitor.com/Business/The-Entrepreneurial-Mind/2011/0228/Female-entrepreneurs-and-the-lifestyle-business.
21. Lorrie Thomas Ross, "Want to Create a Business Lifestyle You Love?" The Story Exchange, June 26, 2018, https://thestoryexchange.org/start-sustainable-lifestyle-business/.

Chapter 6

22. David Gelles, "How the Social Mission of Ben & Jerry's Survived Being Gobbled Up," *New York Times*, April 21, 2015, https://www.nytimes.com/2015/08/23/

business/how-ben-jerrys-social-mission-survived-being-gobbled-up.html.
23. Gelles, "Ben & Jerry's."
24. Marcia Kaplan, "Crowdfunding: 5 Things You Should Know," Practical Ecommerce, November 24, 2011, https://www.practicalecommerce.com/Crowdfunding-5-Things-You-Should-Know.

Chapter 7

25. Will Kenton, "Broker-Dealer," Brokers>Stock Brokers, Investopedia, updated March 29, 2019, https://www.investopedia.com/terms/b/broker-dealer.asp.
26. Electronic Code of Federal Regulations, Title 17: Commodity and Securities Exchanges, Part 227 – Regulation Crowdfunding, General Rules and Regulations, Subpart D – Funding Portal Regulation, § 227.400 – Registration of funding portals, current as of January 23, 2020, https://www.ecfr.gov/cgi-bin/text-idx?SID=e0f938d0a2e3d3817b63f6bc6bbd323a&mc=true&node=se17.3.227_1400&rgn=div8.
27. Crowdfund Capital Advisors, "The 2018 State of Regulation Crowdfunding," report submitted to the U.S. Securities and

Exchange Commission, January 2019, https://crowdfundcapitaladvisors.com/downloads/the-2018-state-of-regulation-crowdfunding/.

28. Joyce M. Rosenberg, "Why Equity Crowdfunding is Not Living Up to the Hype," *Inc.*, May 9, 2018, https://www.inc.com/associated-press/equity-crowdfunding-investing-business-not-working-hype-investors-regulations-sec.html.

29. Jeff White, "CDFIs: The Ultimate Guide to Community Development Financial Institutions," Fit Small Business, April 11, 2017, https://fitsmallbusiness.com/community-development-financial-institutions-cdfi-list/.

Chapter 9

30. "Never Doubt That a Small Group of Thoughtful, Committed Citizens Can Change the World; Indeed, It's the Only Thing That Ever Has," Quote Investigator, November 12, 2017, https://quoteinvestigator.com/2017/11/12/change-world/, (NOTE: in this online reference, no definitive source is named, but concludes that the quote is generally attributed to Margaret Mead by way of

her being quoted in a book by Donald Keys in 1982.)

31. Brian Beckon, Amy Cortese, Janice Shade, and Michael Shuman, "Introduction, " in *Community Investment Funds: A How-To Guide for Building Local Wealth, Equity, and Justice*, ed. Michele Spring-Moore (Northampton: Solidago Foundation, 2020), 12.

32. Chris Horymski, "How Much Does the Average American Have in Savings?" Magnify Money, August 23, 2018, https://www.magnifymoney.com/blog/news/average-american-savings/.

33. George Nurisso and Edward S. Prescott, "The 1970s Origins of Too Big to Fail," Federal Reserve Bank of Cleveland, October 18, 2017, https://www.clevelandfed.org/en/newsroom-and-events/publications/economic-commentary/2017-economic-commentaries/ec-201717-origins-of-too-big-to-fail.aspx.

34. Miranda Marquit, "Too Big to Fail Banks: Where Are They Now?" Investopedia, June 25, 2019, https://www.investopedia.com/insights/too-big-fail-banks-where-are-they-now/.

35. ILSR, "Bank Market Share by Size of Institution, 1995 to 2014," Institute for

Local Self-Reliance, May 14, 2019, https://ilsr.org/bank-market-share-by-size-of-institution/.
36. Stacy Mitchell, "Banking For the Rest of Us," Institute for Local Self-Reliance, April 1, 2012, https://ilsr.org/banking-for-the-rest-of-us/.

Chapter 10

37. "Meet Our Team," Kubé, accessed January 13, 2020, https://www.kubenicecream.com/copy-of-our-story.
38. Kai Nortey, phone interview and email messages with author, October 8-9, 2019.
39. Joseph R. Blasi, Richard B. Freeman, Douglas L. Kruse, "The American Vision," in *The Citizen's Share: Putting Ownership Back into Democracy*, ed. William Frucht (New Haven & London, Yale University Press, 2013), 17-26.
40. Beckon, Cortese, Shade, Shuman, "Introduction," 12.
41. "The Wisdom of Crowds (Vox Populi) by Francis Galton," All About Psychology, access January 27, 2020, https://www.all-about-psychology.com/the-wisdom-of-crowds.html.

42. "About Us," Patriotic Millionaires, accessed January 27, 2020, https://patrioticmillionaires.org/about/.
43. "Home page," Resource Generation, accessed January 27, 2020, https://resourcegeneration.org.

About the Author

Janice Shade is a social entrepreneur, financial innovator, and author with 30 years' experience building brands, businesses, and movements. After an early career in brand management at Procter & Gamble, Welch's, and Seventh Generation, she set out to explore new models for conscious commerce and community capital.

Since 2006, she has launched or cofounded for profit and nonprofit ventures including TrueBody Products, Milk Money, and Local First Vermont, all of which share common themes of democratic access to capital and local economic resilience. Her current venture is The Initiative for Local Capital, a non-profit innovation lab that promotes economic justice for all. She is also a founding board member of the National Coalition for Community Capital.

An avid skier and hiker, science fiction enthusiast, and devoted soccer/ballet mom, Janice lives in Jericho, Vermont, with her husband, two daughters, and their dog, Willow.

www.ingramcontent.com/pod-product-compliance
Lightning Source LLC
Chambersburg PA
CBHW031149020426
42333CB00013B/572